DETOX
YOUR
HEART

"Valerie Mason-John knows trauma from the inside out, and also the practices that can heal and free our hearts. For anyone who wants to engage with emotions in a transformational way, this book is filled with practical and powerful wisdom."
—Tara Brach, PhD, author of *Radical Acceptance*

"This is a book full of heart, which explores with compassion the many layers of human emotions."
—Jackee Holder, author of *Soul Purpose*

"I'm generally not a fan of self-help manuals, but this is something different. This is an author passing on the wisdom of hard experience and showing there is a way to get yourself back on track. Her honesty, warmth, and humanity are a precious and all-too-rare commodity."
—Jenni Murray, BBC's *Women's Hour*

"Offers readers both the inspiration and the insight to work on themselves."
—Christopher Titmuss, from his foreword

DETOX YOUR HEART

Meditations for Healing Emotional Trauma

VALERIE MASON-JOHN

Forewords by angel Kyodo williams and Christopher Titmuss

Wisdom

Wisdom Publications
199 Elm Street
Somerville, MA 02144 USA
wisdomexperience.org

Library of Congress Cataloging-in-Publication Data
Names: Mason-John, Valerie, author.
Title: Detox your heart : meditations for healing emotional trauma / Valerie Mason-John;
    forewords by Christopher Titmuss and angel Kyodo williams.
Description: Somerville, MA : Wisdom Publications, [2017] | Includes bibliographical references.
Identifiers: LCCN 2016030097 (print) | LCCN 2016047974 (ebook) | ISBN
    9781614293873 (pbk. : alk. paper) | ISBN 1614293872 (pbk. : alk. paper) | ISBN
    9781614294030 () | ISBN 1614294038 ()
Subjects: LCSH: Buddhism—Psychology. | Emotions—Religious aspects—
    Buddhism. | Healing—Religious aspects—Buddhism. | Psychic trauma—Religious
    aspects—Buddhism.
Classification: LCC BQ4570.P76 M37 2017 (print) | LCC BQ4570.P76 (ebook) | DDC
    294.3/4442—dc23
LC record available at https://lccn.loc.gov/2016030097

ISBN 978-1-61429-387-3   ebook ISBN 978-1-61429-403-0

25 24 23 22
5 4 3 2

Cover design by Laura Shaw. Interior design by Barbara Haines. Set in Aragon 10.5/14.5.

Wisdom Publications' books are printed on acid-free paper and meet the guidelines
for permanence and durability of the Production Guidelines for Book Longevity of the
Council on Library Resources.

Printed in the United States of America.

Please visit fscus.org.

For all who experience pain and suffering:

Know that there is an end of suffering. Everything changes.

CONTENTS

FOREWORD *by angel Kyodo williams*

We are living in times of great confusion.

Technology not only distances us from one another as we spend more and more hours communicating from behind a screen, but it also brings us together to rally for important causes or reach out and remain in touch with loved ones across thousands of miles of land and sea.

Social media draws us further into the already persistent habit of becoming stars of our own little personal movies. The movies we replay in our heads—held on to from lives past—cause us to recycle stories that no longer serve us, if they ever did.

We run these stories over and over again and like hamsters on a wheel; we go nowhere in our inner life development, and as a result we suffer as adults from the wounds of our childhood.

Slowly these toxic stories crowd out the potential for joy and ease that is the birthright of every human being.

In so many ways, we can point to—and we would be right—the fact that the culture being advanced by Western society is, in an array of ways, increasingly toxic.

Polarization of worldviews seems at an all-time high. Countries and cultures are torn asunder by wars—religious, tribal, ethnic, racial, and of course simply based on greed.

We've been told that our parents didn't raise us right. For many of us, we experienced our families of origin as sources of pain and abuse more so than love and support. Social oppression forces us out into the margins of society, and we are judged or held back by everything from gender to race to religion to our choice of who and how we love.

The transgressions are many and the places for respite can seem few. No wonder we can become burdened and overwhelmed!

As Valerie points out right upfront in *Detox Your Heart*, your thinking becomes toxic from the buildup of anger, fear, anxiety, and confusion. Because mind and heart are one, the toxic thoughts of your mind become the toxic experience of your heart.

However, if we simply give ourselves over to this narrative, to the storyline of "Uns and Nots"—unloved, unseen, unappreciated, unwanted, uncared for, not good enough, not smart enough, not attractive enough, not powerful, not rich enough, not the right color or gender or position or class—then we abdicate the one thing that can reposition our relationship to the entire experience of our life: responsibility.

I often say, "It's not your fault, but it's your responsibility." It is quite true that there are many conditions in life that confer a less-than-desirable experience. But it is also true that at the end of your days on this planet, your life will have been lived only by you. *How you experience whatever conditions life hands you correlates directly to how much responsibility you choose to take.* None of us can control all (if any) of the conditions, but we can choose how we experience the conditions we find ourselves in.

If we do not begin to debunk the deep inner myth that many of us carry that we do not deserve greater joy, love, or ease in our loves because we are _____ (fill in the blank with your choice of Uns or Nots), then we condemn ourselves to the role of victims in our own movies.

Instead of understanding conditions as what may be toxic—but also temporary—your heart becomes the source of what ails.

I originally met Valerie while visiting the San Francisco–based center of her practice community, Triratna Buddhist Community. I'm sure we couldn't help but notice each other, as we are both women of African descent practicing in lineages of Buddhism strongly populated by white Westerners. My own tradition of Zen has also been oriented toward a very male-centered, sometimes even aggressive, expression. The practices can be intense and solitary. Descended from medieval Japan after wending its way from its origins in India through China and Korea before arriving in the West, everything about the practice was unfamiliar: the aesthetics, the flowing robes, small cushions to sit on, folding your knees like only kids do in the West. That kind of environment didn't seem like the kind of place that a twenty-two-year-old, black–mixed race, queer, feminist, and political and social activist woman would decide to find connection to her inner life. But I did. Eventually I became one of very few—there are currently only three—black women sanctioned as teachers in this foreign-from-the-outside world.

In some ways, we are doubly foreign: Buddhism is not from our own heritage or motherlands, and we have largely learned from and among white practitioners. One could say—and people sometimes do—that it doesn't make sense that we would take up Buddhism. But one of the things we share is an ability to see beyond the labels put on things and recognize the essential nature: whatever label you may put on it, teachings and practices that support people in detoxing their hearts of negative thoughts and emotions and unskillful behaviors are teachings that belong to us all. We have enough borders and divisions and imaginations of difference that make us feel separate—not only from each other, but from our own selves. What Valerie offers here are tools and teachings that unify, first and foremost, our minds with our own hearts. Only from there can we truly hope to begin to branch out further to look across the landscape of perceived otherness and see the decidedly hopeful sameness of our shared humanity.

The man that would become known as the historic Buddha, Siddhartha Gautama, was often compared to a doctor. When one suffers deeply, one doesn't question the name of the medicine, but rather one takes it in small doses to see if works to ease the suffering. If the medicine remains in the bottle it is of little use. Similarly, *Detox Your Heart* provides a diagnosis as well as a prescription: practices to treat the ongoing ailment of heart-minds toxified by the environs we find ourselves in. Like the medicine offered by the Buddha, its efficacy—its ability to usher the toxins of our heart out and relieve our suffering—is best proven by direct experience.

Once you receive the prescription, taking the medicine will be up to you.

Rev. angel Kyodo williams
Berkeley, California

FOREWORD *by Christopher Titmuss*

"I became bored and returned to my hedonistic lifestyle of champagne and cocaine." When I read this sentence on the first page of the opening chapter of *Detox Your Heart*, I had the sense that Valerie Mason-John has been through one helluva roller coaster. She writes that she had managed to convince herself to "party all night with my friends and still manage to meet my daily headlines as a journalist."

She goes on to report, "I joked that I had a poisoned brain." That sounded to me like a typical British understatement. Her account of her lifestyle reads like a nightmare! Not an uncommon one.

The opening pages give the reader a clear sense of the prevailing message of the book, that no matter how bad things get, we never lose our potential for a real and lasting inner change that contributes not only to the healing of body and brain but purifies the heart, enabling natural happiness and well-being to flourish.

In the great profusion of books on mind, body, and spirit, the books that carry the weight of authority work well when the author writes from his or her personal experience and relates the all-important and practical stepping-stones toward inner change. The value of *Detox Your Heart* is the equal strength of the personal and the practical. It can't be that easy for a writer, especially a journalist, to be so disarmingly honest about a lifestyle where her consciousness daily obsesses her with the next pursuit of pleasure that fails to get satisfied for more than a few minutes, or hours if she is lucky.

Readers might ask, "Who would want to live like that?" Some people do. Far too many people do. Some seem emotionally, mentally, and physically to get away with it, according to Valerie's perceptions, although it seems to me there is a huge cost to living in such a narcissistic way and in the company of other self-obsessed pursuers of pleasure at the expense of deep love, happiness, and wisdom.

This book is a contemporary classic case study in the four noble truths, the core and irreplaceable center of the Buddha's teachings: (1) There is suffering, (2) there are causes and conditions for suffering, especially being entrapped in desire, (3) there is the complete resolution, and (4) there is the way to resolve it.

Detox Your Heart carries an underlying text of a city dweller living on a diet of sex, drugs, and rock-and-roll (surely the "three jewels" for many hedonists) with inspirational and practical suggestions to get out of this ensnarement. The suffering, despair, and pervasive boredom eventually eat away at the initial pleasures and highs available through the partying life to the point that one feels utterly miserable and in a mess.

How far down do we have to sink before we reach the turning point? In thirty years of teaching, I have been told by some people who have lived through a similar nightmare that at times they believed it couldn't get any worse, and it did. There is no bottom to hell. Nor to heaven. From a Buddhist perspective death is no escape.

Many people in society have completely (and understandably) thrown out all notions that religion has anything to offer. They have settled for career, money, and pursuit of pleasure as the central purpose of existence. Programmed and conditioned in this way, it becomes harder and harder to dig deep enough within to touch on another sense of what life is all about. I can't imagine that any thoughtful human being can become content with the mundane.

There is an understandable attraction for a shift in consciousness, to transform perception, to open the heart and feel a deep sense of connectedness. An ecstasy tablet or a sniff of cocaine may temporarily make the world appear more beautiful and radiant, and offer a cosmic oneness. In time, and often in a very short time, the world of conflict, unresolved personal issues, and the painful depths of dissatisfaction surface, hitting consciousness with a vengeance. This is crisis time. One cannot escape the unresolved through drink and drugs, period. What goes up (including consciousness) comes down, sometimes falling into the pit of self-hatred.

The sharing of drugs, sex, and music does bring about—to put it in the most positive light imaginable—a kind of community of men and women having fun and pleasure together, engaged in often secret and pseudoreligious acts of interconnection. But this world is frequently (though not always) ensnared in fear, paranoia, mafia, sexually transmitted diseases, unwanted pregnancies, and a music industry of greed for profit and mind-boggling egos. One can only ask, and it is important to ask, what on earth has one got oneself into?

Frankly, I can't see religion, counseling, and therapy as the answer to all this, though each in its own way can be immensely helpful. There also has to be some kind of stirring of the human spirit that transcends the limitations of the conditioned and habituated self, and the forlorn plight that it finds itself in. In other words, self-obsession and self-hatred are not only personal crises but spiritual and collective ones.

It's an enormous task to start shifting the priorities away from hedonism and a career, built on the personal desire for money, status, and power, and determine to detox the heart. There is no substitute for inner work and the inner journey. Joining that moving zoo of commuters to and from work in a major city is small change in comparison.

Valerie seems to have taken stock of her distressingly painful situation, examined what she was avoiding in herself—both past and present—and realized that for her the way into heaven would need to pass through the hell of honest self-examination. Her book comprises a link between personal experiences and practical exercises. She details some of the steps necessary to overcome what Buddhists call the multiple hindrance attack, namely, self-obsessed desire, anger, boredom, restlessness, and fearful doubts. To detox (de: remove; toxicum: poison) is to purify the inner life so that generosity replaces greed, kindness replaces hatred, and creativity replaces fear.

I recall going to the home of a wealthy businessman who had invited a number of his friends to meet me for a session of spiritual inquiry. One of the questions I asked a guest was, "If there is one thing you would like to change in your life, what would it be?" His eyebrows rose and he looked up toward the ceiling while remaining silent for several moments, then replied, "Well, I suppose there are lots of things I would like to change."

It was a rather normal response to an uncomfortable question to be asked in front of a group of friends and colleagues. We will often resort to generalities. I pressed home the question. He then said, "My relationship to food." I could literally see why. He wasn't obese, which means more than 20 percent above average body weight for his height, nor was he justifying his situation like the car sticker that said, "I'm not fat. My head is too small for my body." The portly businessman had made the important shift from the generality "lots of things" to the specific: overeating. We need to name the issue. What are the practical steps? Many steps have much in common.

- Be clearly aware of the specific.
- Remember to breathe mindfully through the desire and explore alternatives to the desire.
- Remain one-pointed to overcome the issue.
- Be willing to keep working with the issue on a daily basis.
- Use our imagination to generate change.
- Seek the kind support of others in the process.

As Valerie says, you can overcome your "painful feelings, your irrational feelings, and your obsessive thoughts" that toxify your heart. For Valerie, and others, Buddhist meditation and the practice of mindfulness played an invaluable role in her work to change her habits, codependency issues, and lifestyle. We have to see through our own experience what works well for inner change. Inner peace, contentment, and natural happiness with the ordinary and everyday are our birthright, yet obsessive patterns take us away from such daily experiences.

Valerie's account and practical exercises offer readers both the inspiration and the insight to work on themselves. There are two main issues that contribute to a genuine and lasting transformation.

First, love for oneself. On the face of it, this sounds self-indulgent and narcissistic. We have to think of it in another way. If you have a child or grandchild, and you give this child total attention, then the quality of this attention is an act of love. You will notice that the child responds extraordinarily well to such a quality of attention. This is love. At times, and in the same way, we need to give ourselves such attention as the first major step to detox the heart. Am I willing to give total attention to a specific personal issue?

Second, do I really want to change? Talking with others—whether friends (or even family members), counselors, psychotherapists, analysts, psychiatrists, or spiritual teachers—on any regular basis does not itself reveal a deep, abiding interest to change. It may only be the desire to talk about our issues so that we temporarily feel better during the meeting and for a time afterward. We might even come to believe that inner change comes about as the result of a long, gradual inner process. That view becomes another strategy for avoiding real change.

If we can put our hand on our hearts and say yes to these questions, then we truly move forward as we seek out through our experience the kind of practical exercises to implement a detox of the heart. Our steps may include reaching out to others for wise counsel in either the short term or long term. Change comes about not only through our own efforts but through those of others, some of whom have been through their own particular hell as well.

In the act of reading this book, I hope you will be able to generate some time for inner reflection. Adopting a Buddhist approach, you may be willing to ask yourself, "What do I need in order to give wholehearted attention to myself? What are the causes and conditions that contribute to this toxic heart? What is the resolution? How can I make these changes?"

We can take a "natural pause," as Valerie constantly reminds us. Any invaluable work includes practices to transform our inner life. I can't help remembering what Carl Jung, the Swiss analyst, said to the woman who came to him with an urgent question, "Why are people so mean to me?" Jung replied, "Why are you so mean to people?" We often find ourselves living in a world that mirrors our own states of mind. People may reflect back our own states of mind. Let's not forget, it should add extra motivation to detox the heart!

In the Dharma,
Christopher Titmuss

ACKNOWLEDGMENTS

A Note from the Author for the Wisdom Edition

When Wisdom Publications said they would like me to do a new edition of this book, I of course said yes, not without thinking I am eleven years older and hopefully wiser. I've chosen to update this manuscript rather than make major revisions. Because although I know much more than what I did in 2005, all of what you will read on these pages is still relevant today. If I was to begin writing in all that I know now, it would become a completely different book. In the words of William Shakespeare: "Wisely and slow. They stumble that run fast." There is only so much we can absorb in one book, and the rest can be saved for another.

I have made some corrections, as my understanding of feelings and emotions has deepened, and there are some more stories that I have gathered along my journey that help to bring alive some of the points. I also update my journey of forgiveness toward my mother. Once I thought I resolved it, I lost it. Forgiveness isn't a one-off event; it is forever changing, like everything else in life.

This new edition would not have been possible without the generosity of Windhorse Publications, my first publisher in the UK.

I am grateful for the inspiration of Wisdom's editorial director, Josh Bartok, the generous and wise help of my editor, Andy Francis, and the commitment of Wisdom Publications. Thank you, Wisdom, for inviting me onto your bookshelves. Thank you to Priyananda and Maya Chowdhry, who coached me on the difference between updating and revising a book. And to Dawa Philips for giving me the tip that readers love new stories. And to my partner, Cheryl Kehoe, who is a rock, and my biggest supporter of all the work that I do. She continues to teach me to open up my heart and radiate love to anyone who crosses my path. As best you can, may you all have an undefended heart while joining me on this journey of detoxing your heart. Start from where you are at. That is good enough for the moment of now. And in the next now it will be good enough too.

Acknowledgments from the Previous Edition

First I must thank everyone I have ever met, because these people and many more to come have been and will be my teachers.

My favorite part of any book I write is the thank-you list, because it is a reminder that my friends, family, and readers have all helped by supporting and encouraging me to write. Special thanks go to my "spiritual mother," Maitreyi, for her wholehearted guidance and seeing this book within me. Also to my "spiritual heart surgeon," Ratnavandana, for teaching me how to open up my heart and experience kindness and compassion for myself.

Thank you very much to my editor, Jnanasiddhi, for seeing the jewel in this book when it was first presented as rambling insights, and for helping me craft it into an accessible self-awareness book. Thank you to all my readers for their constructive feedback: Valerie Witonksa, Zehra Balmain, Jo Broadwood, Carey Haslam, Atula, Paramananda, and Theresa Holman. To all the people I interviewed, thank you for sharing your courageous stories. Special thanks go to Jackie Mollison, Lorna Lee Leslie, Georgina Edema, Ratnasuri, Femi, and Panyin. Finally thank you to the Friends of the Western Buddhist Order, Clean Break, Leap Confronting Conflict, and my fellow anger-management trainers.

DETOX
YOUR
HEART

1 🪶 A Toxic Heart

There is the daze—
And then the vacant gaze—
The morning after—
A night of hedonistic laughter—

My Story: Recognizing Toxins

One morning, at the age of twenty-nine, I woke up, held my head in my hands, and cried, "I want my mind back." My head was fuzzed from recreational drugs; my moods rocketed so high that I was too charged to be able to communicate and plummeted so low that I sometimes had to keep myself under lock and key. I could party all night with my friends and still manage to meet my daily deadlines as a journalist, but deep down I knew I had blown holes in my brain. There were gaps of missing information, and I joked that I had a poisoned brain. I didn't know it then, but what I had was worse: a toxic heart.

On waking that morning, I knew drastic changes were needed. I jumped out of bed and did some headstands, hoping the blood would flood to my head and revitalize me. The next day I enrolled in a Spanish class, hoping that learning a new language would massage my mind and help me develop new brain cells. Needless to say, I abandoned headstands after putting my neck out several times, and after investing several hundred pounds in Spanish lessons I became bored and returned to a hedonistic life of champagne and cocaine. This was, after all, what everyone around me was doing, and none of them seemed to worry; most of them seemed to be managing to keep their life together and hold down a job.

Then I discovered Transcendental Meditation, through which I could get high—as I saw it—for nothing. My mental states altered, and for an hour or two my heart felt pleasant, as if it had been purified. Of course I had to come down from the mountain, but I still sensed

3

something had changed inside me. I wasn't sure what it was, but I knew I had discovered something that would affect the direction of my life. Some months later I realized what it was: I had rediscovered my heart. It was toxic, but at last I was back in touch with some of my feelings and emotions.

Looking for a more intensive experience of meditation, and with my meditation teacher having left for India, I went on my first Buddhist retreat with the Friends of the Western Buddhist Order. It was here that I was introduced to meditation practices that led to what are described in Buddhism as the four sublime abodes: loving-kindness, compassion, sympathetic joy and gladness, and psychic integration or equanimity. In each of these meditations I was taught to wish positive thoughts of kindness, compassion, sympathetic joy, and peace for myself, a friend, someone I hardly knew, and someone I didn't like. It proved to be revolutionary.

These practices definitely made me high, but more importantly they put me back in touch with my heart. Just as a clenched fist is gently relaxed and slowly opened as a hand, so my heart started to open, and I could begin to let go some of my toxins: old hurts, resentments, and grudges. It was as though I had been given permission to love myself as well as others, to rejoice in myself as well as others, to give myself—and others—compassion; and I had rediscovered a glimpse of peace within my heart.

I remember thinking when I left this retreat that the world had changed. But it was me: something inside me had begun to open up. I remember walking down the street and smiling at somebody I had sworn I would never speak to again because she had done the "worst thing ever" to me. "What was all that about?" I wondered. Then I realized that only the day before I had been thinking about her in my meditation and wondered why she had wanted to hurt me. During this reflection I realized she might be experiencing feelings of hurt too, so I did my utmost to wish her free of suffering, to wish her well in the world.

Something must have worked, because I hadn't *meant* to speak to her again, let alone smile at her. A few years later she came up to me and apologized, and we were able to speak about that turning point when I smiled at her in the street.

Realizations

Alongside the rediscovery of my heart during this retreat, I came face-to-face with the fact that the same heart that could radiate kindness and compassion was full of toxins. It was as though I saw my heart and how much anger, fear, and hatred was festering there. When I sat to meditate, I couldn't believe how much I was holding on to. I could feel the unpleasant tremors of my anger rumbling in my heart. I felt fear in the body, but I didn't want to let it go. There were people I hated, people I was angry with, and people I had banished from my heart. I realized I had become uncomfortably numb and that I could no longer keep at bay the anger I had been suppressing for many years.

I started to realize that much of my anger could be traced back to childhood conditioning. I began to realize how it had begun to fester. My inability to speak out about my sexual, physical, and emotional abuse had deposited layers of unexpressed, toxic emotions. I had become a victim of my past.

By the age of five I had lived with three families. By the age of eight I had been sexually abused by my children's-home siblings, and raped. At the age of eleven I went, against my will, to live with my African mother. Eighteen months later I was removed by the police and put back in care because of allegations of abuse. By then I had gone off the rails. I was living on the streets by the time I was fourteen, and by the age of fifteen I was locked up in a children's detention center.

When I was seventeen I came out into the world and had to pick up the pieces. I was confused and, although I was fortunate enough to turn to education as an anchor, I coped throughout my late teens and twenties by numbing all my frustrations with the eating disorders anorexia nervosa and bulimia nervosa, partying all night long, and taking recreational intoxicants.

When I did become aware that I was not happy, I just didn't know how to change my life: how to let go of my eating disorders, for example. Books like *You Can Heal Your Life,* by Louise Hay, and *Lovingkindness,* by Sharon Salzberg, became my guides, and I slowly began to stumble in the right direction. I knew I wanted to change. It was precisely this realization that started to open me up to new things and allowed the things I needed to enter my life.

No Quick Fixes

For me meditation was the thing that blew the lid off everything I was trying to keep out of sight. The meditation practice of mindfulness—being aware of every moment—was like having a telescope pointed at my heart. In the light of such attentiveness to myself, I couldn't hide from the fact that my heart was full of anger, nor could I continue to intellectualize or anaesthetize my way through life. I was beginning to have a deeper experience of myself, which I couldn't deny.

But I didn't wholeheartedly embrace the path of transformation offered by meditation straightaway. I was still looking for a magic pill, that easy answer that makes everything just go away. I tried climbing mountains, sitting by the ocean or waterfalls, walking by rivers, taking trips to the gym or into the countryside, running, swimming, and walking, but none of these brought about lasting harmony in my heart. They were only helpful quick fixes to keep my rage at bay.

One thing that stopped me going deeper in meditation was an idea that meditation was just for Buddhists. But after some research I learned that all sorts of people meditate, regardless of religion, culture, or race.

> There's nothing exotic about meditation. It's a birthright of everybody. Animals know all about it. Animals have the capacity for sitting still and tuning in on their own inside consciousness, as well as outside consciousness, for great periods of time. And they can restore themselves by doing that; you can see them doing it. The calmness of deer at rest at midday is the order of meditation. It's a curious thing that Western man has gotten so anxious about it and has forgotten what it is and really looks askance on anyone doing it. Most of the rest of the world knows how to meditate and does so in one way or another.[1]

I relaxed and acknowledged that meditation helped me grasp the fact that I had layers of anger and hatred. Though it didn't instantly detoxify them, it did take away the overwhelming fear of coming into relationship with why I was harboring such toxins. What meditation did was gently slow down my personal movie.

Meditation is *about* slowing down: it is about allowing ourselves to be in the present moment and feel what we are feeling, without judging or punishing ourselves for feeling it.

- First we must have the courage to notice what is happening in our minds.
- Second, we must have the courage to notice and accept that our mind is full of all sorts of distractions—sometimes full of craving and sometimes full of aversions.
- Third, we must have the courage to face our feelings with a calm mind full of kind breath. And have the energy to bring the mind back from its agitated state of distractions, forgetfulness, and mind meandering.
- In essence we must slow down in every waking activity that we do. Meditation is sitting, walking, standing, lying, sleeping, and talking.

When I slowed down I began to rediscover who I was, and what I needed. When I paused, I realized I actually *wanted* to let go of my anger and my pain, but I didn't know how. I began to see that my lifestyle was pushing away my anger rather than helping me let go of it.

I came to see that although drugs, partying, and a hedonistic lifestyle had brought about a type of happiness for a while—often on the basis of mood-altering enhancers—in the long term it led to suffering. I craved being continually high, which in turn led to even more suffering. I was just putting a bandage over my anger hoping it would heal, but instead it generated more fear and hatred in my heart. I knew I had to find a different way to work with these toxins. I could no longer just try to blot them out or push them away. I didn't want to muddle through anymore, internalizing all my anger, just so that I could function in the world as an acceptable adult.

But it was hard to change. I had convinced myself that I was all right. I had this secret illness that very few people knew about, but in the eyes of the world I was a successful journalist, working as an international correspondent, writing books and plays. It was when I stepped inside my home that I fell apart. My eating disorder had become a bat I beat myself up with every day, until one day, when quite literally on the floor, I saw that help had been staring me in my face in the form of meditation and therapy. Once I got over the belief that I didn't have a right to explore my life when there were many other people in the world experiencing greater suffering than I could imagine, I stepped onto the path that would truly allow me to change.

There were many strands to my journey toward compassion for myself and others. My professional career shifted from journalism to the stage; I wrote and performed in plays, and became a television presenter. I also embarked on a personal journey into psychodrama and psychosynthesis therapies, as well as mime and physical theater training. In mime school I reclaimed the art of play, lightening my heart and reliving some lost childhood years.

I kept learning. I learned it was not enough to sit in meditation and wish myself happiness, or keep repeating "I love myself." This all helped, but the destructive "I hate myself" still buzzed in my head, especially at my most vulnerable moments. I had to go deeper; I had to commit to rediscovering myself. And now I know I have to let go of the identities that have constructed the I that hates itself, to find true freedom from the voice that says: "I hate myself, I'm not good enough, I'm unlovable, I'm a fraud, nobody loves me."

There was the danger that attending meditation classes and going on Buddhist retreats would become my new quick fixes. To transform myself, I had to engage the toxins in my heart and explore my anger, hatred, and fear. I had to commit to changing my life, slowly at first, with the escape clause that I could always go back to my old way of being if I wanted to.

I realized that my working life supported my hedonistic lifestyle. Champagne and cocaine went hand in hand with the show-business life of theater, television, and huge open-air festivals. If I was to move toward happiness I had to change the conditions in which I had chosen to live my life, or the cycle of parties, ecstasy, and alcohol would continue to cage me like a hamster going round and around in its wheel. I had to step out of the limelight.

Sharing My Journey

When I opened up to the possibility of change, it was as if new things entered into my life by magic. I embarked on a master's degree in creative writing, the arts, and education, and left my high-flying job. At around the same time I and several other theater practitioners were asked to pool our skills to design a program of workshops for young people with challenging behavior.

The program we developed was a success in every sense. The pilot won funding to deliver the same program in several boroughs in London. And I realized I wanted to help change people's lives by using the creative arts to work with anger and hatred. I committed myself to my own path of healing while helping others explore their relationship to the anger, fear, and hatred in their lives at the same time. I started working with children as young as eight, and adults as old as sixty-five, who all had one thing in common: an eclipsed heart, a heart full of toxins.

At first the people I was working with were people who had hit crises, people society couldn't cope with. They were either in prison or young people's exclusion units, homeless, or attached to a mental health institution. I also wanted to reach out to people who functioned in the world and held down responsible jobs, but who, if they were to slow down, would also find that anger was numbing their hearts. I felt compelled to share my personal experiences of anger, hatred, and fear, and combine them with my professional experience of working in the field of anger and conflict to help them empower their lives. While reflecting on my writing career during a meditation retreat, I realized it was time to integrate my writing into the work I was doing on conflict.

I have chosen to write about anger, hatred, and fear because I have personal experience of them and I continually try to walk a path that will transform them. I also focus on them because they are some of the more common emotions that all of us witness or experience in our lives. If we take the time to look, we can see that they are acted out in our personal lives, in the media, and on a national and international scale, in both subtle and not so subtle ways. It happens in kindergarten, kids teasing each other about how they look, what they eat. It happens in our homes. Statistics show that the most common place for someone to be assaulted is in their own home or in their car. It happens among politicians. "If you don't do what we want you to do we will drop a bomb on you." Hatred, anger, and fear penetrate every sector of our society, and love and compassion can impact every sector of our society too.

Anger, hatred, and fear are not fixed, unchanging parts of ourselves. They are, fundamentally, thoughts with a thinker—thoughts that become toxic emotions and consume our hearts. The mind will produce thoughts. We are powerless over the thoughts that can arise. And we have to accept that sometimes unwholesome thoughts will arise that may disturb us. We have a choice to let the thought arise and cease, or identify with the thought, and begin thinking the thoughts. It's this thinking that stirs the toxic emotions that consume our hearts. We must take responsibility for our thinking. It may seem as if I take the heart and mind to be two distinct things. In fact, they are one, but toxic thinking has split them in two, creating a chasm between the heart and mind. This book is about reuniting the heart with the mind. We do this by cultivating loving-kindness. When we practice loving-kindness twenty-four hours a day, seven days a week, only wholesome thoughts will arise in the heart/mind.

What's in This Book for You?

I make no apology. This is a self-awareness book. "How is it different from all the others?" you might ask. There are many different ways to say the same thing, different paths that lead to the same destination. My aim is that by speaking honestly, from personal experience, what I have to say will resonate with our shared human experience, and thereby will resonate with you. If my words don't resonate with you, I encourage you to stay open and to continue looking for something that does resonate with you. Try to be honest with yourself. Sometimes we fall into the cynical mindset that "nothing is ever right," and this stops us from doing the self-exploration we really need. It is only by really facing up to our inner demons that we can step closer to the inner peace we all long for.

This book is meant to slow you down for a moment and help you become aware of your state of mind. The fact that you have picked up this book and begun to read it means that you are already slowing down and taking a look at yourself. Even if you don't continue reading after this page, take the opportunity right now to acknowledge what you're feeling. It may be that you are not quite ready to explore your relationship to anger, hatred, and fear, or you may not be in the most supportive conditions to do so. It is OK to simply acknowledge this, knowing that at a later date you can always reopen the book and restart your journey from a different point. Before you continue or put the book down, please take one breath with me. One breath can save our lives. When we are aware of our breath it alerts us to what is going on in the body, in the heart/mind.

One Breath

Take one deep breath in and become aware of your body as you breathe out, noting what you are feeling.

- Body Like Mountain: just as a mountain is sturdy, present, and unmovable, allow your body to be sturdy, present, and unmovable.
- Mind Like Sky: just as the sky is wide and open, allow your mind to be wide and open.
- Heart Like Ocean: just as the waves in an ocean arise and cease, let your thoughts and feelings arise and cease.
- Breath Like Anchor: just as an anchor steadies a boat, allow your breath to steady your body, heart/mind, thoughts and feelings.

I draw on a number of sources for the reflections, practices, and meditations included in this book: from traditional Buddhist teachings—though you don't have to be a Buddhist to benefit—to my work as a trainer in anger management and conflict resolution and reflections from my own path. The practical suggestions, reflective exercises, and other well-known meditations are there for you to try if you want to. They are there to help you slow down. However, if you find yourself in the flow of reading, and find the instruction to put the book down irritating, just pause, take three deep breaths, and come back to the exercises when you are ready.

We first of all explore what a heart free of toxins might feel like—freedom of heart—and introduce some of the tools that we will use throughout the book. The next three sections provide a detailed look at the toxins of anger, hatred, and fear. Starting with recounting a little of my own story, we then explore anger, hatred, and fear. What do they feel like in the body? What are some of the overlying emotions attached to them? We will also explore other toxins, like revenge, ill will, jealousy, and envy. How do they manifest in our lives? I emphasize the need to come into relationship with our uncomfortable feelings and emotions, because only then can we learn to work with them, recognizing that these states are impermanent, that they arise and pass away. This is the beginning of being able to let them go.

Each chapter on the toxins is paired with one in which we look at transformation of that toxin. These chapters focus on how we can change. We are not stuck with our emotions or our thoughts—no one is fixed by fate to be an angry person or a fearful person. We can change. Recognizing this, I explore ways in which we can help that change along through reflection and action.

It is best to begin with chapter 2, but after working through that chapter, the other sections on the toxins can be read in any order. Perhaps begin with the one with which you have the most resonance. None of these explorations is definitive or comprehensive; they are personal insights into the states of mind that we all experience.

The art of pausing is the art of healing: we have less conflict in our lives when we slow down—we become more aware of our feelings, and more able to look after ourselves when confronted by anger, hatred, and fear. A key belief running through this book is that we are each responsible for our own attitudes. Yes, there is mental pain, and when we resist it, abscond from it, we begin to catastrophize, and suffering will arise.

Suffering and joy is optional. Has anyone ever told you to cheer up? And you've scowled and said: "I don't want to cheer up, I'm quite happy how I am." This is us holding on to fixed views that cause us suffering. Pausing helps us to respond creatively. When we don't pause, we react; we act without being aware of what we are thinking, or what is being defended in the heart/mind. It has been said that life is about 10 percent what happens to us and that the remaining 90 percent is how we react to things that happen to us. I used to think my life was suffering. And the only way I could end this suffering was by taking my life. Fortunately I learned that my life wasn't suffering at all. It was how I responded to my life that created the suffering. This wisdom saved my life, physically and emotionally. I hope it will save many others from depression, negative mental states, and at worst, thinking the only option is to take one's life.

So good luck. As best you can, embrace what you may discover. Our feelings, our hearts, our bodies, and our minds are the best teachers we could ever come across.

Here is a short fable for you to reflect on before reading any further.

A Fable

One day the heart woke up and said to its mind, "I feel very happy today."

"Impossible," the mind replied. "If you're happy, why aren't I?"

The heart smiled again and said, "Nothing is impossible. At long last I am happy again. I refuse to be poisoned by your thoughts."

The mind shouted back, "It's not fair!"

"Whose fault is it that you're not happy?" replied the heart.

"Not mine," retorted the mind. "I've got a headache, stomachache, constipation, I can't sleep at night, I don't like my job, or where I live, or . . ."

"Pause for a moment," the heart interrupted. "Take a deep breath and slow down."

"Slow down? Are you mad? If I slow down I might never be able to get out of bed in the morning and go to work. You don't have to live my life," the mind fumed.

"It's your choice," the heart replied.

"Choice? What choice have I got? I've got bills to pay and children to feed. It's all right for you."

The heart smiled and said, "And it can be all right for you too. I've stopped going to refuge in your thoughts. They don't dominate me anymore. My happiness will stay. Why don't you welcome me back?"

"No!" cried the mind. "My thoughts will not become homeless. Where else can I house them? If you evict me we'll no longer be one."

"Haven't you realized your thinking has already pushed me away? We are already split. When are you going to start allowing yourself to feel?"

"Feel? Bloody feel? When have I got time to feel?" blasted the mind. "You really are a lunatic."

"You can turn away from your feelings and hold on to your toxic thinking and remain unhappy, or you can pause and let my happiness reunite you to me, your heart. This is freedom of heart."

The mind was speechless. It tried to speak, but instead it paused, took a deep breath, and slowed down . . . 🍂

2 Freedom of Heart

A Fable

The mind thought for a while, then said, "OK, tell me about freedom of heart." And the heart said, "Freedom of heart is the complete union of heart and mind as one. A union that is peaceful, balanced, and happy."

When your mind becomes angry, so does your heart, and all your happiness disappears. When your mind becomes consumed with hateful stories, your heart will be full of hate and all your happiness will be poisoned. When your mind is hemmed in by fear, your heart will be too afraid to open and it will use stories of anger and hatred to protect itself. Therefore freedom of heart is freedom from anger, hatred, and fear. Freedom of heart is freedom from the proliferation of thought—the thinking that creates stories about ourselves and others. Freedom of heart is a peaceful mind, a mind where thoughts arise and cease without a thinker.

If you are to free your heart, you must embrace your painful feelings, and have faith that your thoughts will arise and cease of their own accord. They will pass if you can face them head on, with kindly eyes. Your thoughts and feelings will dissolve if you don't try to hold on to them or push them away. Thinking will dissipate. Trust in this universal law of change.

When the heart is rid of toxins, it becomes a happy heart. A happy heart is an accepting and forgiving heart. A forgiving heart is a contented heart. A heart is contented when it is free of dis-ease and in harmony with the mind.

And remember—your freedom is within.

Freeing the Heart

Our hearts are like the sun. The heart full of love is like the warm orb of the radiant sun in a cloudless sky—it warms, illuminates, and sustains everything it touches. The heart full of anger is like sunlight distorted with a magnifying glass so that its nurturing warmth becomes destructive and harmful, burning up whatever it touches. A heart full of fear is like the sun hidden away behind the clouds; its warmth cannot reach those who need it. When we touch the warmth of loving-kindness that is innate in all of our hearts, our world begins to change.

All of us could become happier—not by winning the lottery or finding the perfect partner, but by believing in our inner capacity for happiness and working to rid ourselves of whatever stands in the way. When we face up to what stands in our way, we start to free up the heart. Paradoxically, we need to be in touch with the discomfort or dissatisfaction that lives within us before happiness can flow through us. We need to be aware that our suffering as well as our happiness is held within our own hearts. When our internal world of emotions has less gravitational pull on us, our external world will change.

Freedom of heart starts with acknowledging and accepting that things in our lives aren't quite right—though we might not know why. This acknowledgment can make space for the realization that we could benefit from more joy in our lives.

Despite what I told you in the brief biography in the previous chapter, if you had known me in my early twenties I would have looked you straight in the eye and told you I was happy and that I'd had a happy childhood, and of course there's some truth in that. I held on to the happy memories to block out the painful ones. But this also meant I couldn't move on. By the time I was in my late twenties I couldn't delude myself any longer; I knew I wanted to be happier. My rock-and-roll life was losing its gloss and I was becoming bored with it all. Boredom highlighted my dissatisfaction and I slowly began to pay attention to the toxins in my heart. It's not enough to hold on to our happiness if we have not let go of our painful past. This is called spiritual bypassing; one day the past will come to haunt us and we will have to face the fact that we can no longer suppress the painful past.

You might say, "You had every right to be angry with your life. Given the magnitude of your hardships and problems, it's no surprise that you later had to attend to your anger, fear, and hatred." But in order to be truly happy, we still need to become aware of our toxins, no matter how small they are, or how small we think they are. If we don't, they will fester and slowly poison our hearts and we will continue to recreate, in subtle or gross ways, the cycle of pain in our hearts, pushing away uncomfortable feelings, letting them accumulate within us and restrict the heart's natural response to be kind—to ourselves and to others. Or we will choose to cling to our toxins, become obsessed by them, and even build our identity around them.

To free our hearts is to understand why we are sometimes angry, why we are sometimes consumed with hatred or plagued by fear. The root of our pain is often the very fear of becoming aware of our toxins—and it is this fear that prevents us from freeing the heart. This fear can be very strong. I used to believe I would be so overwhelmed by pain that if I faced it I wouldn't be able to function in daily life. Instead I discovered that if I became aware of the toxins in my heart, then the anger, hatred, and fear began to dissolve. My heart began to detox.

Looking Within

Allow yourself to go inward for a moment. Consider what kind of relationship you have with yourself. How do you talk to yourself, respond to your emotions, your moods?

Then think about your life and your relationship with others. Is there a connection?

Very often the relationship we have with ourselves mirrors the relationship we have with the rest of our lives. If you leave the house in the morning after an argument, how often does everyone else you come into contact with for the rest of that day suffer? If we are angry with ourselves for something we do, or have done, in our lives, the chances are that we will be angry with others for doing exactly the same thing. If we are ashamed of part of ourselves, we're likely to hate that characteristic in someone else. If we fear something, we see evidence of it everywhere.

Our bodies, hearts, and minds are our home for our entire lives. If we are not comfortable inside our bodies, hearts, and minds, everyone around us is likely to feel the weight of our anger, hatred, or fear, no matter how small it is. By freeing ourselves from within, we also free ourselves from many of the external conditions that seem to oppress us.

Many of us have found external ways to detox our hearts that help to bring temporary calm into our lives. Some of us let off steam by going for long walks in the country, others exercise or go on a sunshine holiday, have sex, treat ourselves to something new, see friends, or climb a mountain. Of course there are many more things you could list, things you do to maintain your sanity in a busy city or stressful life, and to help protect yourself. Honor the ways that you have supported your heart up to now, and begin to open yourself up to new ways—ways that can have far-reaching effects on your life.

Imagine for a moment that we stop looking outside ourselves for happiness, and instead look within: we then lay the way open to discover more joy, peace, and satisfaction within ourselves. While a new relationship, a new job, a promotion, a new home, a child, or money can bring us some happiness, we need to accept that this happiness will not—cannot—last forever in our hearts. Our hunger for something more, our dissatisfaction with life, will arise again. Even if we are lucky enough to have all the money we need, or achieve our ultimate dream, when something happens that triggers our anger, hatred, or fear, our happiness gets extinguished in a flash.

Yet this thing that has triggered our anger or upset might not have the same effect on someone else who has been exposed to the same situation or the same words. So is the cause of our anger within or without? We must begin to own our anger and look within, rather than blaming all the external factors in our lives. I have learned that to get in touch with true happiness I must let go of my expectations. I need to stop looking "out there" for my happiness. The world owes me nothing. This might sound harsh, but it can in fact be liberating. It is at times a rough journey, but it is no harder than the journey we might be in the middle of right now.

To begin the work of looking within, we will need to familiarize ourselves with new skills and tools. Some of the skills and tools we'll be using throughout this book and that, with practice, can free us from the inside out are:

- developing more awareness of what we already know
- developing or enhancing self-love within our hearts
- taking time to pause
- loving ourselves
- connecting with the breath
- feeling our feelings
- reflecting
- repeating affirmations
- chanting mantras
- meditating

Loving Ourselves

Learning to love ourselves strengthens us from within. It weakens the hold that our anger, fear, and hatred have over us. Learning to love myself has been one of my most important lessons. I realized one day that not only did blaming others for my misery, unhappiness, and pain not make me any happier, neither did blaming myself. In fact I became more bitter and angry. It was only when I began to accept myself for who I was, when I started cultivating a more compassionate and kinder approach to myself, that happiness began to trickle into my heart.

Self-love began my process of dissolving anger, hatred, and fear. Admittedly I had friends and therapists to support me in my journey, but in the end I had to do the work on my own. This was the beginning of me freeing my heart.

When I had little self-love, my love for others was toxic: full of expectations, conditions, resentment, anger, and fear. I expected my lovers to love me so much—enough to cancel out my pain. I often became angry and resentful after a few weeks of intoxicating bliss, because my deep-seated pain was still there. I still disliked myself, and I blamed my lovers for not curing my pain.

I loved myself so frugally that I had to place my innate desire to love somewhere else, so I placed it on my lovers. It could then become so obsessive that I sometimes scared myself. I remember, twenty years ago, looking at someone I loved very much and that person saying to me, "You look at me as if you hate me."

I shuddered. They were right. At that moment, I knew no other way to look at them. I hated myself so much that all I could do was love obsessively and with craving. Now that I love myself, I love my friends more, and have less obsession to stifle my lovers. This alone has brought happiness into my life.

You may come to the conclusion that this doesn't apply to you, that you have never suffered from such obsessions. We all have buried resentments and fears that inhibit us. We all sometimes experience irritation, anger, ill will, hatred, or fear. We all have room for more happiness in our lives and could benefit from detoxing our hearts.

The poet Ryokan said, "If your heart is pure, then all things in your world are pure,"[2] which also means that if our hearts are impure, then all things in our world will be impure. When our minds whirl around in destructive thought patterns, we are likely to encounter all sorts of external problems and conflicts. Reflect on this last statement for a while. Is it really that absurd to think this way? Detox your heart, and you will detox your life.

Rediscovering Your Heart

There was a time when I didn't even know where my heart was. I would feel around to see if it was beating. If I was to release the toxins in my heart, I needed to know where my heart was, and I wanted to be able to feel it. I hadn't yet realized that my thoughts were connected with my heart, that while I was thinking I was also feeling.

In Asia, people have believed for centuries that the heart and mind are one, but this was news to me. No separation of the two? Feeling and thinking is part of the same process. The body produces feeling tone— pleasant, unpleasant, neutral, or a mixture of all three. Feeling tone arises out of the eye, ear, nose, tongue, body, or mind having contact with an object or stimulus. And of course from the ageing and decaying body. Feeling tone is unavoidable. Whenever one of the senses has contact with an object or stimulus feeling will inevitably arise. There is no gap between contact and feeling tone. Feeling tone automatically produces perceptions. These perceptions are made up of thought, which creates mental impressions and interpretations. The gap is between the perceptions and mental formations, which are the resentments, the judgments, the anger, the stinking thinking. But we miss the nanosecond of a gap and our attention is captured by the stinking thinking. An overidentification with our thoughts causes them to ossify and become hardened beliefs that we do not want to let go of.

While we cannot control the thoughts that arise in our perceptions because they are so automatic, we are not powerless over our mental formations. They stir up so many negative mental states, which are rooted in craving, conceit and our views. We must become aware of the gap between thoughts that arise in perceptions and the thinking that arises in mental formations. While thoughts stimulate the mind, we do not have to act on them or believe them. We have to learn to have thoughts without a thinker. We lose all peripheral awareness, cling to the thought as if this is our identity, thinking the thoughts, which then creates the toxins in the heart. So when I speak of detoxing the heart, I include the mind in this process.

"There are two minds within the conscious brain: the rational and emotional. This is the so-called head and heart metaphor. It is the tight integration of these two minds that constructs our experience of life," writes a friend of mine in his book, *How to Be Happy*.[3] And Patrick Whiteside tells us in his *Little Book of Happiness*, "Human experience begins in the mind. Human experience dwells in the mind. What of the world outside the mind? There is no world outside the mind. We experience the world with our minds."[4]

Let's take an example to illustrate this. The state of being in love is perhaps one of the most exaggerated emotions that we will experience, so it's a good one to show what I mean. We can experience being in love in our hearts, but this, in turn, has a huge impact on our minds. There is no distinction. When we are in love, our hearts and minds are full of all sorts of heightened emotions, thoughts, and feelings. At times it is as if our whole body has been pumped with a bliss-inducing drug. People tell us how well we look, and we have a happy spring in the way we move, and almost everybody and everything around us is wonderful as we look at the world through rose-tinted glasses, and we attract people. There are moments where we are just love, and people can smell it, see it, and hear it. Our hearts are completely open and undefended. Things change and our hearts shrink and shrivel.

At the other end of the spectrum is anger—another emotion all of us will experience at some time. We feel anger in our hearts, and this too has an impact on our emotions, thoughts, and feelings. Our minds are often full of thoughts spinning with rage about what a person has done, or what we would like to happen to them. We become anger, and people can smell our anger, see our anger, and hear our anger. Anger affects our bodies too, and people keep their distance. Our hearts race, we gasp for air, and our movements become aggressive. At times we are so full of rage that we can't even hear our thoughts or feel our anger. We are often blinkered. The person we are angry with can never do anything right; they are the worst person on earth; we can see things only from our point of view.

Both emotions intoxicate our hearts and fill our minds, and both can leave us exhausted. We can see how our hearts and minds are affected by such strong emotions. Our hearts are literally changed by our thinking. Our thinking influences the personal worlds that we live in.

So anger and love can have a similar effect on our hearts, minds, and bodies, in the sense that these emotions can consume us, we can be intoxicated by our thoughts, and we experience a rush of energy. Some people may even become addicted to the rush of one emotion or both, having reached a point where they only feel truly alive when experiencing such intense emotions. Such people have lost the ability to feel subtler emotions and feelings that can also bring life and energy to our experience. Many of us have lost the ability to feel the subtle sensations of the breath on the upper lip and inside the nostrils. When we connect to the subtle sensations we are no longer waiting for the big-bang experience, and we begin to appreciate and learn from the subtleties of feelings, thoughts, and emotions.

Is it a coincidence that so many people suffer and die from heart disease or dis-ease? The broken heart, the bruised heart, and the sick heart all have an effect on us; they house overwhelming thoughts that dominate the mind. So while the heart and mind are one, they often become split from each other because of the toxic thoughts that we hold on to and/or act out.

There is a saying, "There is no way to happiness; happiness is the way." This means the heart is the way to happiness. If we focused on our hearts, our thinking would detox, our hearts and minds would reunite as one, and happiness would arise.

Slowing Down

 Practice: Pausing

- Pause, then take a deep breath right down into your stomach.

- While inhaling try to connect with your heart, as if you were breathing in through your heart. Then breathe back out through the heart.

- Now connect to the subtlety of breath while breathing in and out through the nostrils; when you breathe in it feels cool and when you breathe out it feels warmer.

- Breathe in like this a couple more times.

- Then take another three deep breaths in the same way, but this time, as you inhale through the heart, breathe in loving-kindness toward yourself, and on the exhalation imagine you are breathing out all your toxins.

- After you have done this, just continue to sit or lie for a few moments enjoying the natural rhythm of your breath.

It was the discovery of meditation that brought more kindness into my heart. Through the practice of slowing down, I discovered a sense of calm and inner space in which I could become more aware of my toxins.

When we are caught up in the busyness of life, it is as if we are on a wheel, spinning round and around with little chance to change anything or respond creatively to life's tests.

When spinning on the wheel of busyness, we might suppress or disguise our emotions—as I did through intoxicants and activity—rather than feel them. Pushing away uncomfortable emotions can help us temporarily. As long as we are successful we can feel better, perhaps even have a laugh with our friends. But it doesn't last and our wheel of life spins even faster.

Whenever an uncomfortable feeling arises, we resist, contract, resent, and hold our breath. Most people will reach out for something external in the hope that we can block it. In this way we delude ourselves that we are OK, that we don't need to change our lives. But we're liable to eventually become unhappy—a victim of addiction, workaholism, depression, isolation, or fiery eruptions. Our wheels are spinning at such a pace that we sometimes don't even recognize ourselves.

Take a minute to try this out: Clench your hand into a fist or clench your toes up tight. Are you breathing normally, or are you holding your breath a bit? For most of us, the breath is a bit constricted when we clench up. This is exactly what happens when an unwanted feeling arises—we tighten up and stop breathing. Clench your fist or foot again, and then let out a relaxed out-breath. When I do this my hand or foot automatically releases a bit of its tension. Intentionally breathing out when we are tense helps us to release our fear and cultivate more calm in our hearts and minds.

Slowing down allows us to see our lives clearly; it gives us options by allowing us to cultivate awareness in our hearts—a helpful alternative to indulging or blocking our feelings. Pausing can guide us through our lives. Meditation is one of the ways by which we can pause and bring more peace into our hearts. Sitting in a meditative position can be a break from the external world and a journey into our inner world. This is one of the places where we can begin to experience calmer and happier states of mind.

Slowing down, through meditation or other means, is also one of the ways that we can begin to connect with the breath. This is important, as the quality of our breath often provides the first warning that anger, hatred, or fear is rising in our hearts. When our minds are calm, our breath is calm; when a toxin disturbs or unbalances our minds, our breathing often changes.

Many of us do not breathe fully, yet without the breath we would not be alive. When I visited a Bodyworks exhibition in London, I couldn't believe the size of our lungs: each the size of a hot water bottle. I immediately started to be aware of my breathing, and how rarely I breathe to my full capacity.

This simple act of becoming aware of my breath, standing in the middle of the exhibition surrounded by strangers, paused the running flow of thoughts and reactions within me. It was a vivid illustration of how attending to the breath helped me to slow down in my full and busy life. In fact I stopped moving with the crowd from exhibit to exhibit and slowed down, allowing myself to take time to explore the exhibition more fully.

Connecting with the breath and engaging in regular meditation can help reduce anxiety and stress in our lives, and bring a feeling of peace to our hearts. However, if we are to use meditation to work with the toxins in our hearts, we must remember the real work is when and how we are engaging with our regular world.

Practice: A Breath Practice

- Pause for a moment.
- Feel your feet on the ground and your buttocks connecting with your seat.
- If you are lying down, feel your body being supported by the bed or the ground.
- Connect with the breath and take three deep breaths. Then pause.
- Now follow the unique rhythm of your breath. Try not to affect it, just continue to be aware of it for five more minutes.
- Then become aware of the present moment, experiencing what is happening right now in your heart, in your mind.
- Try this practice during your day, when you first wake up, at midday, and before you sleep. Even if you are on your feet all day, just stop and take three deep breaths, and notice the effect.

If we can do this practice even once a day, it will make a difference to our hearts. We will begin to create natural pauses in our waking life, instead of rushing from one thing to the next without thinking. Taking a deliberate breath slows us down; it can also help us to become aware of what we are feeling. When we pause, we come more into relationship with our bodies, minds, and hearts. If we then do this practice every hour, our lives will start to change. We will slow down and become more aware of what we are thinking and feeling moment by moment. We will then have more choice about how to act on these thoughts and feelings.

Conscious breathing slows us down. As we live in a world that frequently demands the opposite, it is a precious gift.

We live as though there is no time to breathe, no time to feel. We often don't even have time to know what we are experiencing because our lives are so filled with making money to pay the mortgage or the rent, the bills, and buy food for the family. Some of us don't pause from the moment we get up, either forgetting to eat or eating on the hop, finally stopping only when we flop into bed last thing at night. So we need to pause, to be aware of our breath, to slow down, and allow ourselves this gift.

Feeling Your Feelings

People say we can't help how we feel. It's true we can't help unpleasant, pleasant, or neutral feelings arising when one or more of the six senses have made contact with an object. We multiply the intensity of feeling every time we move away from something pleasant or unpleasant; we create a vicious cycle of craving and aversion.

Often when people say we can't help how we feel, they are talking about their emotions. We can help how we experience our emotions. They are created by our unconscious and conscious thinking and conditioning. When we emote our thoughts we are habitually responding and reacting out of our emotions. We are forcibly changing our emotions all the time, by reaching out for external stimuli, or by blaming others when we feel vulnerable or upset. Before we know it, we are angry, resentful, self-righteous, and begin to inhabit a storehouse of toxic thoughts, which suppress our uncomfortable feelings of vulnerability.

If we are patient, our feelings will change of their own accord—some quicker than others. Our emotions will begin to deplete; they won't dominate us, or dictate our behavior. Eventually toxic emotions will disappear and nontoxic thinking will start to arise in our hearts, and one day there will be just thoughts without a thinker. There will be sounds without a hearer, tastes without a taster, smells without a smeller, sights without a seer, and touch without a toucher. What I mean by all of this is that things will arise and we will not identify with them as me, mine, or I. There will be no judgments, interpretations, or stories about what we have just perceived. We will see the bigger picture, and not be caught by the clash of the senses, not react to whatever we have made contact with. We will feel the unpleasantness, pleasant-ness, neutralness, or even the mixture of all three feelings, and will turn toward it without an agitated mind. The heart and mind will accept all of it without protesting. When we protest, toxic emotions begin to emerge.

I can hear you saying: "I love my stories; life will become boring." Yes, we need to make sense of things, but we have to realize that it's not fact, just us thinking through the haze of conditions and experiences. My life has become more joyful since I've begun to drop the pilot, the controller of stories that caused mayhem in my life.

Our hearts well up with toxins because we push away our painful feelings. Many of us will do our utmost to push them down. We won't allow ourselves to stop. Our busy lives don't seem to give us time to feel our feelings. When we turn toward our experience, we will often find feeling tones or sensations in the body. We turn away from the expe-rience in the body with thoughts and thinking. If we have the cour-age to face the feeling tone, we will discover there is nothing there, no I or me, just a flow of sensations that may be painful, pleasurable, or neutral.

Sometimes it is only when I arrive home after a long day that I real-ize something at work has upset me. The end of the day is often the first time I stop and collect myself for long enough to be aware of what is going on.

For example, I have opened up my email and a friend has written: "Sorry V, I can't make it tonight. I'm caught up in work. Let's make another date next week." I've reacted, and immediately sent back a reply: "Forget it. You're always canceling. You just don't care about our friendship." There are many times I've received emails from friends canceling a date and I've taken a breath, which has acted as a hand brake on sending an email like the one above. I've come back the next day, felt much calmer, reread the email, and noticed I didn't even see the bit where she says let's meet up next week. I've responded: "OK hun, sorry not to catch up last night, I was looking forward to it. Yes let's make a date next week."

Let's look at what was going on for me when I didn't take the pause. I read the email, my senses of the mind and eyes have contact with the words, and an unpleasant feeling arises in the body. Sadness and thoughts begin to arise that I'm not even conscious of: "She doesn't care, she doesn't love me, she's always doing this." I begin to identify with these thoughts, thinking these thoughts and stirring up the emotion of anger. This all happens in seconds, and before I know it I have interpreted it as my friend not caring about the relationship and sent a harsh email back.

In a world without pauses, reacting can be a familiar way of communicating, especially when we feel under pressure.

We often tell ourselves there isn't time to sort stuff out because there is a job to be done; there is no room for feelings at work, at home, on holiday. Where can we have our feelings? The reality is that my feelings take up space. Unable to be with the sadness of not seeing my friend, I identified with the sad thoughts, which turned into angry thinking. My friend was upset and reacted with a harsh email back. We sorted it out, and if I had sent the second email, I would have gotten a kinder email back from my friend and we would not have had a conflict to sort out. I have said in the past: "I'm feeling quite sad now." Whenever I have named the sadness I've received warmth and compassion. When I hide the sadness, people can only see my frustration, resentment, and passive-aggressive communication disguised in sarcasm, or passed off as humor.

Many things can block us from really feeling our feelings—not just lack of time. Bad habits, childhood conditioning, the real or perceived expectations of others, the pace of life, or just not being very good at spending time with ourselves—any of these can get in the way. I used to run away from pleasant feelings. No matter if it was pleasure from having a wonderful day, or pleasure from a nourishing meal, or pleasure from enjoying the taste of fine wine. I found it difficult to stay with the pleasurable feeling of being held or touched. Unconsciously I told myself pleasurable feelings were associated with being dirty and worthless. Pleasurable feelings made me feel vulnerable. And so I hated feeling vulnerable too. This story had emerged from childhood when I was sexually abused. There were times when my body had the sensation of pleasure. I hated myself for feeling the pleasure. I told myself it was my fault I was sexually abused. I know now today that when the body is touched in a particular way, pleasant, unpleasant, neutral, or a mixture of all three feeling tones will arise. That is what the body does when it has contact with a particular kind of touch.

It's not surprising that many of us are unaware of what we are actually feeling. Take anger: one dictionary defines anger as "extreme displeasure, inflamed and painful." Just five words to explain a state that can have a lasting effect on our lives. However, our anger is more complicated than this. It is often the disguising of, or the front for, a whole range of feelings, some of them surprising.

Some of us have even learned to deny positive states of mind. We can become confused when a positive feeling or emotion arises, cataloging it as bad or inappropriate. Positive feelings may also feel unsafe: we can become angry or fearful when we experience them. Some people feel they don't have a right to such positive emotions. Some people experience excitement and joy as risky and out of control. They can become anxious and undergo symptoms like sweating or a racing heart, similar to their experience of anger. It has taken me a long time to accept that it is perfectly OK to feel good inside my heart and experience positive states. I can say I love myself without telling myself I'm being self-indulgent, and allow myself to be happy without saying I don't deserve to be.

Instead of connecting with what we may actually be feeling, we have become experts in judging ourselves, often harshly, and in explaining away our experience. So, when we do become aware of what we're feeling, we can become critical of ourselves. We can interpret a feeling so quickly it becomes a judgment about how we are. For example, if we have unpleasant feelings of vulnerability we can criticize ourselves by calling ourselves wimps, or untogether, and say to ourselves, "Get a grip!" These putdowns cause anger, hatred, or fear. These emotions are the acting out of our toxic thoughts.

The chain of events is: first, the facts of what actually happens, then our feelings about it, and then our thoughts. If the thoughts are toxic, judgment swiftly follows, normally in the form of a critical voice inside our heads. Then we negatively interpret what we believe caused the vulnerable feelings, losing all sight of the initial feeling. Before we know it the toxic stories we tell ourselves contaminate our hearts with anger, hatred, or fear, creating a chasm in our hearts. We end up acting them out aggressively, either verbally or physically, or we seethe inside, causing ourselves more harm than good.

Let's take another personal example. Fifteen years ago I was walking along the road and my attention was captured by a letter I had received earlier that day. "Miss Mason-John, while we enjoyed your application, we had so many candidates for the Arts Bursary that we are sorry to tell you that your application was unsuccessful this time. Thank you for applying." My thinking went into a spin as I remembered the letter, and five minutes later I burst out laughing and said aloud, "I can't blame my mother for that." Let's look at what happened.

- The Fact: Remembered the words of the letter that told me my application had been unsuccessful.
- The Feeling Tone: Unpleasant—in the neck, throat, and jaw.
- The Thoughts: "It's not fair. What's wrong with me. Nobody cares. I hate myself." (Identification of these thoughts becomes thinking and I stir up an emotion.)
- The Thinking (interpretations and judgments): It's all my mother's fault, if she had loved me, it would have been different. If she had looked after me I wouldn't have to be begging for money. If she had not abused me I would be more successful in the world. (Hence my stories begin to unfold.)
- The Emotion: Sadness mixed with anger.

Fortunately I caught myself in the story and stopped walking, paused, and hence the laughter came, and then more thoughts. "I can't blame my mother for that. How long am I going to keep on blaming my mother for things I don't get?" The awareness of this stopped me from acting out by turning to a distraction to stuff down my sadness and frustration.

This was a great epiphany that helped me to begin uprooting old stories that had kept me in a rut. Let's look at a generic example. And then you can try one for yourself.

- The Fact: Our partner or a friend says the relationship is over.

- The Feeling Tone: Unpleasant all over the body.

- The Thoughts: "It's not fair. Why me. I'm unlovable. I'm not good enough. I've been abandoned."

- The Thinking: I bet s/he is seeing someone else. If they are I'm going to stalk them and make their life hell. I hope they are as miserable as me. Nobody is going to leave me like this. It's not fair. Who do they think they are?

- The Emotion: Sadness mixed with anger and rage.

- The Actions: We beat ourselves up. We blame ourselves for the loss of the relationship. We begin to act out with our choice of distraction. We isolate.

- What We Gain: Temporary relief.

- What It Costs Us: We become depressed, angry, and resentful for a long time. Relapse into our choice of distraction. Begin to overeat or over drink. Dwell in negative mental states.

Now fill in the blanks for your own example:
- The Fact (What happened): Make it clear, concise, and clean.
- The Feeling Tone (Where you feel it in the body)
- The Thoughts
- The Thinking (Interpretations, judgments, stories)
- The Emotions
- The Actions (What you did or what you do)
- What We Gain (What you gain from your actions)
- What It Costs Us (What your actions cost you)

In a situation like this we accuse them of abandoning us, interpret their actions as personal rejection, and get angry. Our unpleasant feelings of loneliness have become toxic; in fact we are most probably not aware of our loneliness because we have moved into a place of blame. The reality is that underneath the anger, we are most probably feeling, deep down, incredibly lonely, sad, and fearful. We are hurt, and our needs are not met.

The problem is that this thought process can take place in seconds, and before we know it we are screaming insults.

The organization Leap Confronting Conflict describes this process as a vicious circle. There are the facts of what happened, then the feelings, then our toxic thoughts (our interpretations and judgments). We often act these out (verbally, physically, or silently), which may achieve some gains, but the consequences of our actions often outweigh these. After this first cycle, the initial facts that upset us become irrelevant, the facts are bypassed, and our feelings and toxic thoughts get us stuck on this cycle, going round and round, becoming more frustrated each time. We rarely allow ourselves just to be with the actual feeling; instead we quickly describe our experience through judgments, interpretations, blame, or by verbally attacking another person—all of which starts poisoning our thoughts. Unfortunately the person on the receiving end of this can see only our anger, and the conflict starts to escalate.

Whatever our stories, it is a fact that many of us have become expert self-critics, skilled at denying both positive and negative feelings. The fact that we label unpleasant feelings as negative and pleasant feelings as positive is the issue. Unpleasant sensations are judged, pushed down, and numbed. Pleasant feelings are labeled positive, and we grasp and cling onto them, and crave them. We are playing a game of sensations; a pendulum in our minds swings to and fro between the emotions of aversion and craving. If we faced the sensations without labeling we would experience the sensate energy of aversion and craving in our body, and have a choice whether to act out of these emotions or not.

We have come to identify our feelings through our emotions, judgments, and interpretations. The actual feelings are what lie behind all these. So we have become experts at confusing our feelings with our judgments and interpretations of situations and people. Although this has given us a language with which to try to express ourselves, this way of perceiving our feelings also leads inevitably to more conflict. Nobody likes to be judged.

Learning to articulate clearly how we feel is a lifetime practice. Often people confuse feeling with thinking. For example, I can ask a mentee or client, "What are you feeling?" They respond with: "I feel betrayed. I feel judged. I feel that nobody is listening to me." These are not feelings, they are interpretations and stories about a situation. It's imperative for us to begin to realize this, because when we name something "a feeling" we can have the tendency to hold on to it tightly. Nobody can take away our feelings. And the irony is, feelings do not have views that cause us much suffering. We must begin to distinguish between feelings and thoughts, so that we can begin to observe that our thoughts are not facts, and that we do not have to become our thoughts.

Finding a language for our feelings is difficult. Buddhists believe there are only three types of feeling: pleasant, unpleasant, and neutral (I include a fourth feeling that is a mix of these three). This is because "feeling" refers to feeling tone in the body. So, for example, if I am walking along the road and somebody screams, "Hey nigger," I feel the vibration in my body and it is unpleasant. You may well have just felt the vibration too as your eye and mind had contact with the N-word. When I am waiting on the road for a taxi, and I watch taxis stop for all the white people, I begin to have an unpleasant feeling in my body. I move away from the feeling by creating the story that taxis only stop for white people. I then experience anger, which is more pleasant to feel in the body than sadness because it is energetic. You don't have to believe this theory that there are only three or four feelings. But see for yourself what happens when you begin to locate feeling in the body as a physical sensation. By limiting ourselves to these four basic feelings, it becomes much easier to see how much of what we thought of as "feelings" were actually emotional responses derived from stories, interpretations, views, biases, delusions, and judgments. If four feelings is incredibly difficult, please add sorrow, hurt, and happy. And know that the feelings of sadness and hurt are unpleasant in the body. So the story of the unpleasantness is I am sad, or I am hurt. Similarly feelings of happiness are pleasant in the body, and when we feel pleasant we can tell ourselves the story that we are happy.

Sometimes we hold on to the story of sadness and miss the sensation of pleasant when we have eaten a meal, or when we have been surrounded by pleasing aesthetics. This is why I have not included them as feelings; they are stories about a sensation we are experiencing in the moment. Now that you know that, you can choose to add these three or more to your list of feelings. It's your process; this is my understanding of feelings today, and in five more years it may be different. So I cannot reiterate enough to start where you are. Be kind to yourself and see if you can experience the sensations of breath in your body.

Practice: Reflecting on How We Might Feel

Below is a list of descriptions of how we might feel, and a list of interpretations and judgments that can be linked with our anger, hatred, and fear. See if you can add any of your own; this is important, because many of us have a language that belongs to our cultural background and suits us better than standard English.

Try to empower yourself by circling the emotions that you recognize, and try to add other words to the list. This is the beginning of getting back in touch with feelings in the body that you may not have allowed yourself to experience fully for a very long while. See if you can recognize some of the familiar judgments and criticisms we all make, and then perhaps find another word on the list more appropriate to what you are actually feeling. A judgment or interpretation is often a thought. Our thoughts begin to weave stories of being got at. "Blame, insults, putdowns, labels, criticism, comparisons, and diagnoses are all forms of judgment."[5]

Four Feelings (Feeling Tones in the Body)

Unpleasant • Pleasant • Neutral • A Mixture of All Three

Mental Formation (Emotions, Judgments, and Interpretations)

Abandoned • Abused • Afraid • Agitated • Aggravated • Aggressive • Alienated • Alarmed • Aloof • Angry • Anguished • Alarmed • Aloof • Annihilated • Annoyed • Anxious • Apathetic • Apprehensive • Ashamed • Attacked • Bashful • Betrayed • Bewildered • Bitter • Bored • Brokenhearted • Bullied • Burdened • Cautious • Cheated • Cheerful • Coerced • Cold • Compassionate • Concerned • Confident • Confused • Cool • Co-opted • Cornered • Cross • Curious • Dazed • Dejected • Depressed • Despondent • Disappointed • Discouraged • Disgusted • Disillusioned • Dismayed • Disoriented • Displeased • Distressed • Disturbed • Downhearted • Dull • Ecstatic • Embarrassed • Enthusiastic • Envious • Evil • Exasperated •

Excited • Exhausted • Fatigued • Fearful • Forlorn • Fragile • Frightened • Frigid • Frustrated • Full • Furious • Gobsmacked • Grateful • Greedy • Grief-stricken • Guilty • Happy • Hazy • Helpless • Hesitant • Hopeless • Horrible • Hostile • Hot • Humiliated • Hungry • Hurt • Hysterical • Impotent • Indifferent • Innocent • Intense • Interested • Insomniac • Invisible • Irate • Irked • Irritated • Jealous • Jittery • Kind • Lazy • Lethargic • Listless • Lonely • Loved • Love-struck • Mad • Miserable • Misunderstood • Moody • Mopey • Naked • Nauseated • Negative • Nervous • Nettled • Neutral • Numb • Open • Overjoyed • Pained • Panicked • Paranoid • Powerless • Proud • Puzzled • Regretful • Relieved • Reluctant • Resentful • Restless • Revengeful • Sad • Safe • Satisfied • Shocked • Shy • Sorry • Split • Stranded • Stubborn • Sure • Surprised • Suspicious • Tearful • Tense • Thoughtful • Tired • Tranquil • Undecided • Unhappy • Unheard • Unloved • Unnerved • Upset • Uptight • Vexed • Violent • Virile • Vulnerable • Withdrawn • Worried • Worthless • Wretched • Zapped[6]

You might be thinking this is so overwhelming and confusing after reading such a list of feelings, interpretations, and judgments. Behind each of these lurks a story and/or a view that we are holding on to. These labels create fixed identities for ourselves and others. When we begin to see through these labels, we begin to lighten our heart/mind. To reiterate: feeling is sensation or feeling tone in the body. You can have the feeling tone of unpleasant in the body and label it with the emotions of excitement or sadness. You can have the feeling tone of pleasantness in the body and label it as joy or ill will. Or you can have the feeling tone of neutral and label it as boredom or anxiety. So our emotions come into fruition when we label one of the four feelings with an emotion or interpretation.

 ### Practice: Accepting Feelings

- Become aware of your body.
- Take a deep breath in and as you breathe out become aware of your feeling tone: pleasant, unpleasant, neutral, or a mixture of all three.

- Take another deep breath and as you breathe out become aware of any labeling, thoughts, or stories arising.

- Take one more deep breath and expand it throughout the whole body, becoming aware of peripheral sounds, sights, taste, smells, touch of clothing. And pause. 🍂

What often happens when we come into relationship with one of the above feelings is that we try to change what we are feeling because it is uncomfortable or because we believe we shouldn't have such feelings. In denying our feelings we tend to push them down, and this is what causes a feeling to become a toxic emotion and to fester away in our hearts.

Emotions don't have to be negative; they are in fact thoughts arising in the mind that become intense mental activity manifested through thinking that give us some pleasure or displeasure. Emotions like happiness, excitement, joy, love, gratitude, and kindness are important to cultivate. We all have desires; it's when we keep on feeding our desires, chasing after our desires, clinging to our desires, that the toxicity arises. We can begin to tell ourselves we have been "cheated, hard done by" when we don't feel positive emotions.

If we could accept that our feelings, thoughts, and emotions will change just like the weather—if we could walk out of our homes in the morning and just say, "The sun is shining today" or "The rain is raining today"—our lives would become more fulfilling. When we call the sun shining "a beautiful day," we get upset and even angry with the weather when the rain comes. We could be like this with our feelings: oh, an unpleasant feeling has arisen, and now there is a pleasant feeling. And one day we will begin to see no difference in the pleasant, unpleasant, neutral, or mixture of all three. There will be just feeling and we will begin to see the empty nature of the feelings and emotions. When we label them, we give them form, we cognize them, and they begin to have a life of their own. Left alone they arise and cease of their own accord.

We could reread the above lists and place all the emotions, judgments, and interpretations under one of these categories of pleasant, unpleasant, neutral, or a mixture of all three. Emotions, judgments, and interpretations can also arise when we try to push away an unpleasant feeling or cling to a pleasant feeling and crave more, or when we become neutral and ignore what is going on. Our responses of fear and anger are things that have helped to protect us and even motivated us in the past.

However, if we don't push our feelings away, cling to them, or ignore them, we will become aware of how our feelings can change in the space of one day, as an experience of several different feelings. Perhaps you could flick back to these lists after reading each chapter and see if, and how, your feelings or interpretations have changed. We'll see later how, even if our feelings don't seem to change, we can change our thoughts. It is our toxic thoughts that poison our hearts and get us into trouble.

Practice: How Are Your Thoughts and Emotions Running Your Life?

Let's explore this list in more detail. There are the three traditional types of feeling: pleasant, unpleasant, and neutral. "Feeling" refers to feeling tone in the body; it is a sensate experience. We may have more than one feeling at a time, even a mixture of all three, as sometimes we can feel pleasant in our hearts but experience unpleasantness in another part of our physical body. Anything else we are feeling is really what we are thinking. For example if we feel abandoned we are actually thinking that we have been abandoned. If we feel intimidated we are thinking that we are being intimidated. If we are feeling emotionally hurt, we are thinking that someone has hurt us that way. If we are feeling sad, we are thinking that we are sad. Sadness is an emotion and it is real, and it comes with a host of sad thoughts.

The feeling tone gives rise to thoughts, and thoughts create emotions. Usually when we are in touch with any of the three feelings we react by swiftly naming or labeling them with thoughts, which become emotion, judgments, or interpretations. So let's see how they run our lives. The basic pattern of feelings and reactions to them is as follows:

Feeling tone: Unpleasant tone in the body
Reactive thoughts: I am feeling abandoned; I'm being intimidated;
Something is wrong with me.

Feeling tone: Pleasant tone in the body
Reactive thoughts: I want more; I don't deserve this; What if I lose him/her.

Feeling tone: Neutral tone in the body
Reactive thoughts: I'm bored; What's the point?; I can't be bothered.

It is often easier to notice the reactive thoughts than the feeling tone. So we will begin with the reactive thoughts.

When you become aware of your reactive thoughts, like thinking that you've been abandoned, ask yourself the following questions:

- What story am I creating in my mind?
- What interpretations am I making?
- What judgments am I holding on to?
- Am I ready to let go of the story?
- Am I ready to let go of the judgment?
- Am I ready to let go of the interpretations?
- How true are the beliefs I have been holding on to?
- How have the beliefs caused me misery?
- Can I see how I have been creating the extra suffering in my life?
- What am I going to choose to do?

Whatever you choose to do, just accept you have made that choice with some awareness. You can always make a new choice if you need to.

If you are not ready to let go of the story, judgments, and interpretations, ask yourself the following questions:

- Why am I holding on to the story?
- What do I gain from holding on to the story?
- What do I gain from holding on to the judgments?
- What do I gain from holding on to the interpretations?

- What has holding on to the story cost me?
- What has holding on to the judgments cost me?
- What has holding on to the interpretations cost me?
- Can I see how I have been creating the extra suffering in my life?
- What am I going to choose to do?

Now spend some time to sit with your answers. Maintain awareness of your mental actions, and ask yourself if this extra baggage of story, judgment, and interpretation is something you want to keep carrying around.

Let's practice looking at these types of reactive thoughts in more detail by considering some real-world examples. I will write examples in the first person. Notice where I write "I feel" and ask if it is a feeling tone in the body, an emotion, or a story.

Pleasant Feelings

Trigger: I see someone I am romantically interested in.

Feeling tone: I feel pleasant.

Reactive thoughts: They fancy me; They must like me; I feel in love.

Are these thoughts true? I feel like they are: my heart is pounding and I'm tongue tied when I see them.

How do I know it's true they fancy me? Well, I saw the way they looked at me!

How true is all of this? If I am totally honest with myself, I don't really know.

Is there a story in this? Yes. I saw the person, they looked at me in a certain way, and I took it to mean that we are in love.

So what are the facts? I feel very pleasant when I meet the person I am romantically interested in.

Now ask yourself: Can I stay with this pleasant sensation without turning away from it with a thought?

Say to yourself: "As I breathe in I feel pleasant; as I breathe out I feel pleasant," and sit with the pleasantness without reacting. Perhaps allow laughter or tears to dissolve the emotions that can emerge from experiencing pleasantness in the body.

What we learn by practicing in this way is that we can feel sensations in the body without having to react.

Unpleasant Feelings

    Trigger: My friend forgot my birthday.

    Feeling tone: I feel unpleasant.

    Reactive thoughts: She always forgets; I feel abandoned; Nobody cares.

    Are these thoughts true? I feel like they are: she forgot my birthday a couple of years ago, and if she cared she would have seen it was my birthday on Facebook.

    How do I know it's true that she always forgets? I don't actually know that.

    How true is it that I have been abandoned and nobody cares? If I am honest with myself, it's not true; some people do care about me.

    Is there a story in this? Yes. A friend forgot my birthday again, I felt hurt by it, and took it to mean that I have been abandoned and that nobody cares about me.

    So what are the facts? I feel very unpleasant when my friend forgets to wish me a happy birthday.

    Now ask yourself: Can I stay with this unpleasant sensation without turning away from it with a thought?

    Say to yourself: "As I breathe in I feel unpleasant; as I breathe out I feel unpleasant," and sit with the unpleasantness without reacting. Perhaps allow laughter or tears to dissolve the emotions that can emerge from experiencing unpleasantness in the body.

I have given you two examples in the first person. Now choose an example of your own—something that triggers reactive thoughts—and work through the same process of noticing, identifying, and investigating your reactions.

Trigger: _____

Feeling tone: _____

Reactive thoughts: _____

Are these thoughts true? _____

How do I know they are true? _____

How true is it that . . . ? _____

Is there a story in this? _____

So what are the facts? _____

Now ask yourself: Can I stay with this _____
sensation without turning away from it with a thought?

Say to yourself: "As I breathe in I feel _____;
as I breathe out I feel _____," and sit with
the _____ without reacting. Perhaps allow
laughter or tears to dissolve the emotions that can emerge from
experiencing _____ in the body.

Sit with the sensate feeling without reacting with thoughts as best you can, and trust what emerges. Surrender to what happens without naming the feeling. When we surrender we must learn to just sit in the manure of feelings. Manure is fertile and much can grow from this compost. We can grow and change too. It's not what people do to us that matters, it's what we make things mean that matters. This is what causes us misery.

When we let go of needing to be right, we begin to see that every thought we have ever had is a figment of our imagination. We can never say hand on heart, this thought is true. We can never wholeheartedly trust our thinking. All we can do is directly experience everything happening as it is happening. Just as we can savor every taste of a beautiful meal and be completely in the moment with our senses, we must learn to savor every nuance of our feelings, if we want freedom from the prison of our minds.

One day you may actually ask yourself, why do I need to react at all? So I'm feeling unpleasant, pleasant, or neutral in the body. So what? It's just sensation. It's just energy. Why do I need to react? Why do I need to turn away from it with thoughts, thinking, or with any other distraction?

It's a practice. We let our attention focus on the feeling, and we also open up the aperture, so we can see more than the feeling. We are not just our feelings. There is always so much else going on. If the feeling is overwhelming we have most probably teetered into reactive thought.

When we are aware of this we may look at the ceiling and become aware of the room we are in, or we may look up at the sky if we are outside. Become aware of sounds, smells, tangibles, sights, and tastes, so that we are not captured by our thoughts. And when we are able to, we turn back with the breath toward the feeling tone in the body. We may have to do this several times. Every time we catch ourselves identifying with our thoughts or thinking, we look up and expand the breath throughout the whole body. We connect to the senses and expand the breath throughout the whole body. The breath is a hand brake on thinking. 🍃

Freeing Your Feelings

While working as an international correspondent covering the land rights movement in Australia, I had the opportunity to live traditionally with the Yolngu tribe in Arnhem Land. I arrived during the second week of a funeral. The women sat round the burial pit, and breathed almost as though they were chanting. They hit their heads with rocks, and fell to the ground wailing. The men, on seeing the dead body, would breathe, scream, and dive on top of the body wailing too. Everyone who knew the person had the right to grieve, and the body was not buried until everyone had arrived to pay their last respects.

This funeral lasted three weeks, with people freely expressing anger, sadness, and helplessness throughout the whole period. Some people were worn out from grieving; but my overall impression was the sense of beauty, love, and happiness that flowed from their hearts once the funeral was over. There seemed to be no anger, resentment, or hatred—just an acceptance that this person had now passed over to the other side. The mourners had paused, broken away from their daily routine, and given themselves time to breathe, feel, and grieve. They had found a way to express their emotions in a creative, contained, and safe way, without suppressing or numbing them. There was no blaming, just the expression of the unpleasant feelings aroused by the death.

Although the Yolngu way of grieving might be far from our own personal experience, it throws light on how we in the West deal with death, and with emotions generally. I've known people who have died, and, in complete contrast to the example above, I have tried to hold back my tears through fear of losing control. I've worked with colleagues who have lost somebody important to them, and once they return from a few days of compassionate leave, nobody mentions the bereavement. I also have Caribbean and Irish friends who attend wakes where they sit with the dead body for seven days and nights. But even they often numb their feelings with alcohol or other substances.

When we hold back our feelings, or numb them, they don't really go away. They just transform into blame—with statements like "it's not fair," "why me?"—or into anger and resentment. We carry all this in our hearts, deep down, buried among the embers of pain—and we become miserable.

No matter who we are, we will suffer; this is a universal fact. If we didn't fear our suffering so much, it could help us to free our hearts from anger, hatred, and fear. If we were able to accept that we can have many different feelings in one day, and that in the same day we will have the loss of many feelings—that feelings of happiness, or sadness, will cease; if we can trust that there is no need to move away from the feelings we don't like, or stuff them down, that they will come and go of their own accord—we will begin to loosen our attachment to our feelings and thoughts.

If we were less attached to our feelings and thoughts, negative thoughts of animosity would be fleeting. They would perhaps arise— for example at a time of loss—but they would dissolve with our acceptance of such loss. But all too often we are unable to sit with the pain of our loss. Many of us are unable to accept that our happiness has been temporarily thwarted.

Our reaction to loss is one of the main causes of our suffering. Loss of the feelings of happiness is pertinent to all our lives. All of us will experience some form of loss, and ultimately experience the loss of somebody we are close to, through death or other separation. In each instance we can lose touch with the painful feeling itself and instead tell ourselves that we have been abandoned. When feelings associated with abandonment arise it can be as if our body, mind, and heart are too small for all the feelings. Rage, anger, hatred, and several other emotions can take over our lives to the extent that we act out our emotions and vociferously demand justice, compensation, apology, or an explanation of our loss. All of this conjures up the story that we have been abandoned when in actual fact what has happened is that somebody has died, or told us the relationship is over. Unpleasantness arises in the body and we label it abandonment.

There is much negativity in the world, and every individual has his or her part to play. If we want to change the world, we have to change ourselves. In changing ourselves, the world will become a different place. There is a famous line attributed to Mahatma Gandhi: "We must be the change we want to see in the world." Positive change begins with self-love, self-esteem, and self-worth.

It is when we value ourselves that our hearts become free, more open to other people and to change. The toxins that have split our hearts become impotent, and freedom of heart begins to come into action. Our hearts cease to be split from our minds. The tension of anger, hatred, and fear leaves our bodies. We move with more lightness, our faces become more open, and a smile appears on our face. Smiling opens up our hearts even more, allowing kindness toward ourselves and others to flow with ease.

I once visited Plum Village, home of the venerable Thich Nhat Hanh, the Vietnamese Buddhist teacher, in the French Dordogne. In this village of mindfulness he introduces visitors to the practice of smiling. I was astounded to discover how little I smiled, and how much of an effect smiling had on my heart. It just seemed to naturally open me up.

What would be the effect if we all smiled at least once a day? An unconditional smile of warmth and love can be a radical act. We often walk out of our front doors and hardly nod to our neighbors. We pretend we can't see them and hurry along to our destination. A genuine smile is like magic. It opens our hearts and for a few moments releases all the toxins. The practice of smiling can free our feelings and revolutionize our hearts.

 ### Practice: A Smiling Practice

- Just try, for one day, smiling at anyone you come into contact with. If this feels daunting, just give away a smile a day for a week, and note what happens. If you feel a change in your heart, why not adopt the practice of smiling?

- During this practice, try to find your playful self, rather than criticize. The aim is to let your heart smile.

Detoxing Your Heart

Our hearts could be described as huge muscles that open and close, shrivel and expand, soften and harden, love and hate. We have to work diligently to keep our hearts open, just as we have to work to keep other muscles in the body strong. Purifying our hearts is an ongoing process, like physical exercise. It is, as the poet Galway Kinnell writes, necessary to "reteach a thing its loveliness."[7]

When we start to open our hearts, we start to uncover ourselves to ourselves, removing layers of frustration that have become toxic. The way to uncover ourselves is through awareness of our thoughts and emotions. If we are to detox our hearts, build up our heart muscles, and become happier, we must cultivate mindfulness in everything we do. Kahlil Gibran says in *The Prophet* that we must trust in the seasons of the heart. I say we must trust in the seasons of our feelings, observing them come and go like spring, summer, autumn, and winter. With the presence of awareness we can see there is no need to hold on to or push away our thoughts, feelings, and emotions. They will come and go of their own accord. If we push them away or cling to them they will stay in our hearts and accumulate. Similarly, if we allow our thoughts to be like clouds in the sky, they will pass. Even the dark, heavy clouds eventually pass.

How is your heart feeling today? Awareness begins in the heart. This turning inward can be a revolutionary act. We might ask ourselves how we feel when we wake up in the morning. If we know we're feeling unpleasant in the body, we can at least be forewarned. OK, we are feeling emotionally under the weather. Turning toward this feeling in the body may prevent us from becoming angry. Befriend your feelings and see them as a warning to take care of yourself throughout the day. Try not to eradicate or block the experience. Only acknowledge them, then let go. Let the muscles of your heart soften, let your tears dilute your toxins, let the heart stay open.

If you remember, ask yourself in the middle of the day how your heart is. This will help to keep it open, and you may find that what you were feeling in the morning is quite different from what you are feeling at midday. This is impermanence: the universal law of change.

I know from my own experience that suffering is part of life; accepting that everything is in a constant process of change can be the beginning of a new life. I went for a walk in the snow with my nine-year-old foster sister. She was delighted to see big icicles hanging from a nearby bridge. She broke one off and said, "I'll keep this and take it home so everyone else can see." I smiled and we continued our walk in a nearby field. Half an hour later she stopped in her tracks and said, "Look, it's all gone. It turned to water and now there is nothing." I smiled again and said, "Yes, there is nothing there."

We can all remember a time when we lost our tempers, only to wake up a week or a month later and say, "What was all that about?" Our emotions and feelings eventually dissolve—just like the icicle. If we enter a healthier relationship with our feelings, they too can melt and become as nothing. There need not have a lasting negative effect. If our core was truly happy, any feelings of anger, ill will, revenge, or delusion would also feel different. They would be fleeting like gentle winds, and any ill will would eventually dissolve into unconditional love.

This, then, is true freedom of heart: a heart that cultivates only love—indiscriminate, compassionate, kind. Even if anger, hatred, or fear arise, the potency of a loving heart instantly melts the toxins. When we break our attachment to anger, hatred, and fear our hearts are completely liberated and our freedom of heart is abundant.

But before we reach this ultimate liberation, we can develop much freedom in our hearts. Let's begin to explore and understand our toxic emotions. Having rediscovered them, let's discover new ways of working with them, not by pushing our negative emotions away or by clinging to them, but by recognizing them, coming into awareness of them, understanding them, and finally being willing to let go of them. This will put us on the liberating journey of detoxing our hearts.

We must filter our hearts, flush out the poisons, and begin anew.

 Practice: A Heart Practice

Finally, I offer you this heart meditation. You can do this while traveling or relaxing at home. You can do it for five minutes or half an hour. I often do this while traveling on a train or bus, and I am always astonished by how the people around me become more human. I find myself smiling and I'm greeted by friendly smiles too. If I am delayed it helps me keep calm, and not feel anxious about being late. If you are new to inner reflection or meditation, I suggest you begin with just five minutes. You may find you connect with the visualization part of the exercise more than the repetition of phrases, or vice versa. This is OK, as both techniques are beneficial in helping us to slow down and connect with our hearts.

While reflecting on this practice be aware of the pace of your heart. You might find it beats very fast. This often happens when you contact challenging feelings. Don't panic; pay attention to your heartbeat and this will help quiet the breath and the heart, gently slowing them down. When you become more confident, just see how long you naturally want to sit for. Remember to try to notice any difference in your day when you introduce these reflections.

1. Either close your eyes or keep your vision directed slightly downward. Imagine your heart as a dark, mysterious, unknown but beautiful cavern. Imagine the daylight pouring in, and the sunlight opening up and detoxing your heart. Be aware of your breath as you reflect on this beautiful image for two minutes, and become aware of the feelings that arise.

2. Next say to yourself, "Breathing in, I feel my heart, breathing out, my heart is opening." On the next in-breath say, "I feel my heart," and on the following out-breath say, "My heart is opening." Repeat these statements for the next couple of minutes, becoming aware of the feelings that arise.

3. Try to end with the following: say to yourself, "Breathing in, may my heart detox, breathing out, my heart is detoxed." Then on the next in-breath say, "May my heart detox," and on the following out-breath say, "My heart is detoxed." Repeat these statements for one minute, becoming aware of the feelings that arise.

4. Slowly become aware of yourself sitting, wherever you are, connecting with your buttocks, your feet, your hands. If your eyes are closed, gently open them and come back into the world. 🌿

Things to Try

- Take the minimum of three deep breaths throughout your day; perhaps one when you wake up, noting the feeling tone in the body, one before lunch, noting feelings, thoughts, and emotions, and one at the end of the day, where you expand the breath throughout the whole body

- Develop or enhance self-love within your heart by appreciating yourself daily
- Take time to pause
- Connect with the breath
- Lean into your feelings with the breath, aware of smells, sound, taste, touch, sight
- Connect with your heart
- Smile
- When you wake up bring to mind the people you will see in your day. This includes at home, work, on Skype, Google Hangout, Twitter, Facebook, and in person
- Become aware of thoughts
- Catch your judgments and interpretations
- Become aware of change

3 Let's Talk about Anger

A Fable

And the mind said, "Tell me about my anger."

The heart said, "Your anger is a temporary state of thinking or behaving. When your pride is hurt it often becomes your anger. Your hurt pride wants to protest. You have not been heard. You demand to be listened to. Your anger is your inability to feel what is going on for you in the present moment. It is the disguising of your vulnerability. Your anger has been pushed into your heart. Your anger springs from a minefield of suppressed feelings. It is the corruption of these suppressed feelings. Your anger is the explosion of all those suppressed feelings that have never been fully expressed. Anger is the toxin from which hatred arises. Your anger is energy gone overboard—EGO. Your anger is the separation of your heart and mind."

My Story: Recognizing Anger

I had convinced myself that my childhood had been happy. This was the story I told my friends. But deep down I thought the world owed me something. I was waiting for the mother and father I never had. I was angry at having to grow up in orphanages, foster homes, on the streets, and in young people's lockups. I was angry that some of my friends were dead before they reached fifteen.

I wanted my childhood and adolescence back so that I could live it differently. I wanted an apology from all the adults I blamed for ruining my life. I was angry at men and black women, as both had physically and sexually abused me. I saw how the layers of frustration and pain had piled up in my heart and turned to self-hatred. By the time I was thirteen I hated myself so much that I tried to kill myself. My anger had become full-blown self-hatred. I tried again at eighteen. I developed anorexia, which became extreme bulimia nervosa—stuffing and purging food—as a way of coping with life. I denied my feelings, in fact I was so afraid of feeling that if a whiff of unpleasantness or pleasantness arose I would purge it by vomiting. Both feelings would swiftly turn into vulnerability, and I ran half a mile from such emotions.

Whenever I did get in touch with the overwhelming rage at my past, I told myself I had a right to be angry. It gave me the excuse not to take responsibility for myself. I was still searching for someone to look after me—giving me the excuse for my irresponsible lifestyle in my twenties, and always looking to my friends for guidance.

That's how I began to live life in the fast lane—I found friends with whom to party all night. I smothered my rage with traveling, drugs, sex, and rock-and-roll. I went through my twenties in complete protest, deliriously unconscious—although at the time I would have said I was happy. The signs of my unhappiness weren't hard to see, however. I went down to eighty-four pounds, secretly binged, vomited up everything I ate, and took uppers to keep myself happy. I was desperately sad. I had lost the ability to make myself heard—I had lost the ability to express how I felt. I couldn't even cry. My tears became a tight knot in my throat. The only thing I could do for relief was yawn. It eased the knot in my throat. Some years later, I realized why I'd been yawning. "A yawn is a silent scream." When I read this quote on a pin board I smiled, and yawned again.

My first separation, from my biological mother at the age of six weeks, had a huge impact on my life right up to my midthirties. Every time someone left me, whether a carer, teacher, friend, or lover, I interpreted it as a rejection. The ironic thing is that I often manipulated the situation with my lovers so that they would leave, because I believed it was my role in life to be left. I myself didn't know how to leave, so even when I wanted to, I would push the other person away so that they would eventually leave.

I often destroyed everything tangible that reminded me of them, so that I could annihilate them from my life. I couldn't see that my rage was blocked energy.

When I learned to see myself as the fuel for my anger, I began to see how my conditioning affected my experience of life and was part of my rage. My low self-esteem, resulting from my experience of abuse, is part of me, part of the fuel. As a child I decided, consciously or unconsciously, that the reason I didn't grow up with my biological family, the reason I had so many carers who came and left, was that I was unlovable. I carried this heavy burden into my thirties. I was unaware that my internal putdowns were just pushing anger deeper into my heart. They had become life sentences. I can see clearly today that I'm often not actually angry with a person or situation; I'm angry with myself for feeling such unpleasant sensations. My anger takes me away from the lethargic, intense sensations in my throat and belly that I don't like feeling.

Naming Our Anger

Anger has no class preference, no age limit. It is not limited to one gender, culture, race, or color. It is everywhere. Every one of us has experienced some kind of anger, whether a subtle, fleeting moment of annoyance, a lowness from anger kept locked tight inside us, or a volcanic rage. Some people act out their anger, others push it out of sight, but whichever strategy we choose, we end up with disharmony and conflict.

It is not until we can stop pushing away or acting out these feelings and instead come into relationship with the angry part of ourselves that we can begin to dissolve our anger. Other unowned, unnamed feelings often lie behind our anger, such as sadness and fear. These stagnate inside our hearts and get expressed through toxic thoughts of anger and blame: "it's unfair," "it always happens to me," "I'm no good," and "it's their fault."

If we are unable to recognize our true feelings, then our physical, psychological, and spiritual selves get out of sync, and all sorts of maladies can occur. Anger influences our lives. The toxin of anger can poison our experience—whether we're avoiding it or enacting it.

You might think you don't get angry, but before you decide this section doesn't apply to you, let's look at some things that can make people lose their cool—a list that might help you widen your definition of anger. The following is a list of things that women have said makes them angry.[8]

- being bullied or criticized
- being pushed or shoved in a crowd
- being cheated
- being ignored or treated as though I'm stupid
- being kept waiting without being given a reason
- being lied to
- being put down
- being mocked
- not being believed
- being insulted
- being sexually harassed
- being patronized
- being let down
- having my space invaded
- not being given information
- having something taken from me
- being made to look a fool

The list of things that can lead to anger is long, and the ways we express our anger are many. Some of them we might not previously have seen as expressions of anger. For example, when we are angry we can become silent and unable to articulate our feelings. Some people get sick instead of angry; others begin to hear voices. Some people become accident-prone; others become depressed.

Getting to Know Our Anger

Connecting with Our Bodies

When we are angry a whole host of vulnerable feelings percolates into our hearts. These are so physically uncomfortable they feel as though they are choking us, and all we want to do is move away from them rather than sit with them until we feel something else. Our aversion to such feelings can be so strong that we believe we need brute force to push them down or purge them. In fact, I have come to realize that, if we can experience all the levels of what we are feeling, and then have the courage to acknowledge and sit with them, our uncomfortable and vulnerable feelings will not get a chance to fester in this way, and in time they disappear of their own accord. Instead, we often use anger as a distraction from what we are feeling deeper down. Then we end up holding on to those very feelings we fear and avoid—until they become poisonous in our hearts.

So what happens in our bodies when we experience anger? First there is the trigger or the event, then comes the moment when our bodies are invaded by painful, prickly, tense, tearful—even itchy—feelings. These can feel so uncomfortable that we instinctively try to push them away.

The body is a great teacher, so it is important to recognize what is happening in our bodies. Sometimes our bodies become so tense we don't feel they are ours anymore. We can shake, get sweaty armpits, groin, and palms, feel stiff in the neck or shoulders, find our hands making fists, heart beating faster, and so on.

Alternatively, when we are angry we can become so disconnected as to be completely numb to ourselves, our feelings, and everything around us. We can't hear ourselves think or breathe. Our feelings get lost, and we create a wall around us, not letting anybody in. Our anger keeps everything and everybody out. We can't listen to anybody, or even consider another point of view, and some people have out-of-body experiences.

In response to these feelings, a critical voice often steps into our minds and tells us (in our own vernacular) that it's ridiculous to be feeling so vulnerable; it tells us to grow up, or get a grip. Our bodies become tense during this process of trying to push down the feelings, and we feel tight—most commonly in the throat, jaw, shoulders, fists, stomach, and bowels. Our bodies tense up in order to choke back the feelings that make us feel vulnerable, shaky, and tearful. But instead of becoming lighter and calmer, our bodies feel heavier and pumped up with adrenaline.

I asked a group of young men aged between sixteen and twenty-five what happened to them when they became angry, and found their descriptions were the same as those of the women I have worked with, and also reflected some of my own behavior when I became angry.

- I feel out of breath or choked
- my heart beats faster
- my voice becomes high or shaky
- I have dangerous thoughts
- I clench my fists
- I raise my voice
- I wave my hands about
- I make myself bigger
- I grind my teeth
- I can't hear or see anybody else
- I lose control

What do you experience when you're angry? See if you can add to this list.

Watch yourself the next time you're angry. Get to know what happens to your body. Try not to be afraid of your vulnerability; see if you can stay with it, without it overwhelming you. Watch the sensations in your body. How long do they last? Are there stages you go through? Feelings are energy, and they evaporate if we trust that they will arise and cease of their own accord. We maintain the lives of our feelings by attaching them to another person, to ourselves, or to objects. Watch yourself the next time feelings of anger arise; see what you do with them and see what you attach them to.

 Practice: Exploring Physical Sensations
- Sit comfortably in a chair, or lie down on your bed with the soles of your feet on your mattress and your knees pointing to the ceiling.
- Let your breath just be; don't force it. Breathe in and out, enjoying each breath no matter how shallow or deep.
- Become aware of your whole body, beginning with your toes. Clench them, then relax.

- Move up to your ankles; clench, and then relax. Then your calves.
- Move through your body, clenching and relaxing the different parts one at a time: knees, thighs, groin, and buttocks.
- Bring attention to your lower back, then your abdomen.
- Move up to your middle back.
- Now focus on your chest, your upper back, then your arms and hands.
- Breathe into your neck, then finally your face and head, clenching and relaxing the muscles.
- Then just remain sitting or lying and become aware of your whole body. Begin to explore physical sensations as you become aware of them. Become aware of where you hold tension in your body.
- Ask yourself what your body is feeling right now.
- Don't make a judgment, just connect with the physical feelings, whatever they are—itching, tingling, aching, hot or cold, tight or relaxed.
- And remember to breathe. Breathe into the parts of your body where you feel the most physical sensations, and say, "Breathing in I feel physical sensations, breathing out I let go of physical sensations." 🌿

Connecting with the physical sensations in our bodies in this way can be a strong practice. When we pay attention to our bodies, we are beginning to connect with our inner feelings. Anger is energy, and it becomes alive and toxic when we turn away from the unpleasantness of it in the body by projecting it internally or externally.

We give our feelings longer life by attaching them to ourselves, others, and inanimate objects. These feelings often turn into toxic stories and become emotions that poison our hearts. If we just sat with the thoughts of anger, paying little attention to them, they would not attach to anything, and the thoughts of anger would cease of their own accord. It is a practice of patience. When we get attached to our thoughts, stories like "She's intimidating me" or "He's disrespecting me," they hook us and stir the wrath of anger.

In an ancient Buddhist text called the *Dhammapada* the following quote reminds us how harmful it is to attach and identify with our thoughts.

> "He insulted me, she hit me, he beat me, she robbed me"—
> for those who brood on this, hostility isn't stilled.
> "He insulted me, she hit me, he beat me, she robbed me"—
> for those who don't brood on this, hostility is stilled.
> Hostilities aren't stilled through hostility, regardless.
> Hostilities are stilled through nonhostility: this, an unending truth.
> (Verses 3–5)

I have found that learning to sit with our feelings and thoughts without holding on to them, without pushing them away, without chasing after them, and trusting that they will cease, is the best teaching of all.

By becoming alert early on to the fact that our body is tensing up, or becoming numb, we may be able to take preventative action. We can try to relax physically and see what effect that has on our emotions, take a few deep breaths, and slow down our thoughts. Taking deep breaths has delayed me from acting unskillfully and allowed me to pause, preventing me from saying something or sending a text or instant message that I might regret.

Another strong reason to take note of our bodies' messages in this way is that our anger can manifest in more extreme forms. Most people who work in alternative therapies have found a link between anger and a number of physical illnesses and life-threatening diseases. I realize now that the back and shoulder ache I used to get was connected with my anger. I have no more pain, and when I feel my shoulders tense up I tell myself to let go. Engaging with our anger involves coming into relationship with our bodies.

Growing Up Angry

> *They fuck you up, your mum and dad.*
> *They may not mean to, but they do.*

—Philip Larkin, "This Be the Verse"

Starting Young

Looking back I can see that I grew up angry, and I can agree with Philip Larkin, but I must also take responsibility for my own actions. My family conditioning definitely had an effect on who I am today, but there was the choice: I could still be in the maze of institutions, or living the life I have now.

Families differ in how they display anger. Some families argue, others bicker or have occasional flare-ups. In some family homes there is a lot of high emotion and even violence, while other families, on the surface at least, just don't seem to do anger at all. But anger can also be manifested silently, through not communicating, being absent emotionally or physically, or through depression.

Anger is often feared, so some parents act quickly to repress, control, or deny it in themselves and in their children. These children become adults and reinvent the same neurosis, unthinkingly passing these negative opinions to their own children. Children who grow up in these families learn to stifle their emotions at an early age. Looking beyond anger, we see that not only do some children never see their parents argue, they never see them upset or crying. Many children learn from an early age that crying, or being upset, is not the done thing. Being strong, and dealing with pain and sadness "like a man," whether you are male or female, is highly valued in some families. Some children grow up with adults telling them, "If you don't shut up I'll give you something to cry about." This reprimand can only teach a child that its tears are not welcome. "Parents should always be conscious of the fact that they themselves are the principal cause of neurosis in their children."[9]

While parents often pass on neuroses to their children, they cannot be responsible for the outcome of their offspring. There are so many factors that can influence our children, like teachers, celebrity athletes and actors, the internet, and the media. The world is no longer a timely wonder for our children to discover; they can find out everything by a click of a button or a touch on their iPad and iPhone screen. Even if we were fortunate enough to have a happy childhood, the reality is that every one of us, by the time we are five, will have experienced something to be angry about. Our first separation from one or both our parents, our first broken toy, our first scolding, or the first time we are refused something are some of the many times we might feel the heat of anger. At this age our main means of communication is through emotional outburst. If a child is not allowed to act out his or her strong emotions in a safe environment, they will usually become toxic in some form and he or she will soon find another way to express them.

Of course there is also the world around our families affecting us as well. The experiences of growing up, what teachers and other adults say to us, our religion and culture, and the beliefs and values to which we're introduced all have an effect on how we cope with our feelings.

Many lessons learned in childhood, such as criticism and judgment from parents, carers, or teachers, are unknowingly internalized. These become the critical voices, the putdowns in our heads that repeat, or interpret, our parent's or carer's or teacher's words: "It's all your fault," "You're useless," "Stop being such a baby." This inner voice is what I call the "alien," because it invades our minds and contaminates our hearts with all sorts of negative chatter. It alienates the heart from the mind. It fuels our minds with messages: "I should never show my feelings," "I should have gotten it right," "I should be perfect," "I always get it wrong."

When we are children these can become all sorts of reasons, concocted in our heads, for why we might be unlovable. These beliefs stay with us—though not always consciously—into adulthood. They can leave wounds that, when unwittingly reopened, unleash our anger. There is so much in the child's world that is never explained by adults; why things happen, for example. It is left to our fertile imaginations to try to work them out. It can be hard for a child to trust his or her instincts, especially when adults do not allow children to fully express their feelings after a trauma.

Because of this, some children develop what is called "magical thinking," a type of paranoia that tells them that mummy or daddy is ill because of their misbehavior. Or they begin to interpret the trauma as, "This happened because of me, it's all my fault," because it is safer to cope with self-blame and putdowns than with reality.

For some people the putdowns may be the reason they gave themselves for the death of a sibling or parent, or when daddy or mummy walked out of the family. For others, putdowns might come the first time they lose a best friend to someone else. Whatever the reason, the judgment or interpretation we put on our past will begin to eat away at our hearts.

Self-blame and putdowns stock our hearts with toxic thoughts, and by the time we are adults, anger is rumbling away. We need to pay attention to and take care of the vulnerable wounded child that we all have inside us.

The Different Faces of Anger

The Explosion

When James Watt, who invented the first practical steam engine, was a young boy, he took a teakettle, filled it with water, plugged all the openings, and tied on the lid. Then he put it on the fire. Of course as it got hotter and hotter the steam pressure rose and the teakettle finally exploded. This is exactly what happened to me. I was the teakettle, meditating on my cushions with all my feelings stuffed down and corked up, and after a few months of bubbling away in blissful heightened states, my anger, hatred, and fear came to the surface and I finally exploded. I couldn't keep down my toxins any longer.

In the field of anger management there are traditionally two models of how we as human beings contain anger. There are the bottlers, who do "in" anger, and the volcanoes, who do "out" anger. I was a bottler, pushing everything down and screwing the lid on tight, in the hope that even the strength of twenty elephants wouldn't be able to unscrew it. I didn't disclose my past to anybody until I was in my late twenties; in fact, people assumed I came from a privileged background. I was successful at presenting a front that I had nothing at all to be angry about.

The Bottler

Are you a bottler? You might be a bottler if you act out one or more of the following.[10]

- avoid anger
- be polite
- withdraw
- walk away
- stay inside

- seek revenge
- ignore people
- say, "I'm OK, I'm not bothered, I don't care" when thoughts of resentment are rumbling around in your mind
- drink, smoke, use recreational drugs
- not eat, overeat, eat compulsively, binge, or purge
- often use antidepressants, sleeping pills, painkillers
- fall asleep, get headaches or migraines
- take it out on the wrong person
- scratch, cut, or burn yourself to take it out on yourself
- sulk

Bottlers are people who hold their anger in, travel with it, go to bed and wake up with it. Their anger has become a piece of rotten luggage in their hearts, weighing down on them, causing their shoulders to sag. They're often passive aggressive, and disguise criticism in sarcasm or humor. They say, "It was a joke," when the words they have clearly expressed display some discontent.

Many people who bottle their anger will say, "I'm not angry. What are you talking about? I never get angry." Some of these people never actually pop the cork of their bottle; instead they become depressed, perhaps using food, alcohol, or work to help stuff back down the discomfort in their hearts. Eventually, some of these people become like the teakettle, exploding when the pressure finally becomes too much.

Bottlers often see anger, when it finally pops out, as something separate from them. It is as if some living being has jumped inside them and made them angry.

"I don't know what came over me," "I can't believe I got so angry. It's just not like me," "I only get angry when I've been drinking," "I'm not angry, you're the one with all the anger, it's your issue, not mine." These are some of the statements bottlers will come out with.

Some bottlers are so expert at swallowing, repressing, and suppressing their feelings that they believe they never get angry. But they are always at risk of erupting into a fit of rage. Some bottlers put their anger on ice, and become completely detached from their feelings. They have convinced themselves that anger is something that is not part of their lives.

Bottled-up anger is highly toxic and can become depressive, as well as explosive, and eventually cause ill health. Ailments like boils, constipation, migraines, and tension that causes backache or slipped discs can all be associated with the bottler.

The Volcano

Are you a walking volcano? You may be a volcano if you act out one or more of the following.[11]

- channel anger outside yourself
- criticize, or put people down
- deliberately wind others up
- raise your voice when someone disagrees with you
- be sarcastic
- interrupt
- be aggressive, threaten, argue, shout
- break things
- stamp your feet
- pull your hair out
- push and shove
- throw things
- get into fights

Volcanoes walk around with anger bubbling away in their stomachs. Their responses are like reflex emotions. Do you remember when we were children and the doctor tested our reflexes by tapping a hammer on our knees and our legs would automatically fly up? This is what often happens to those of us who walk around like murmuring volcanoes: somebody says the wrong thing, and we fly off the handle.

These are the people we have to tiptoe around through fear we will provoke their anger. They always want their own way, but they don't own their anger and, like the bottler, they claim they don't have a problem; it's everyone else who has a problem. Volcanoes walk out of meetings, slam doors, lash out, bang things about, smash things, use harsh language, and are often unable to listen to anyone else's point of view. Alternatively, these people can be extremely cold in their communication while seething deep down inside.

These people are sometimes called exploders, because their angry responses to situations are immediate, as if they are vomiting all their anger out of their hearts. But the toxic residue of anger still swirls around inside them, lying dormant until the next thing comes along to trigger an explosion.

Ailments associated with this type of anger include insomnia, addiction, backache, ulcers, and irritable bowel syndrome.

Of course, we can oscillate between the two types of anger and have all the ailments too. What didn't upset us yesterday upsets us today.

Conventionally, women tend to be bottlers and men volcanoes. Women are perceived to do "in" anger, holding on to it, taking antidepressants, and becoming more depressed. Men are perceived to do "out" anger, going down the pub, getting drunk, and causing criminal or physical damage. As children, young girls are often told not to be angry, and boys are encouraged not to cry. But between both sexes you will find those who bottle their anger and those who erupt like a volcano.

To Express or Not to Express?

There are many different views on anger and whether it is, as some people claim, a completely normal, healthy, human emotion or, as others claim, an unhealthy and completely useless emotion. The reality is that, whether we believe we have healthy anger or unhealthy anger, it still needs to be transformed, because either type can become destructive.

Anger can be cathartic, inasmuch as feelings build up inside us and need to be released. The force of trapped feelings needs to be expressed. But all too often this comes out in destructive behavior, in the form of putdowns, criticism, depression, or verbal or physical violence. Therapists sometimes encourage the expression of anger through what has been termed "venting." This is the stage of enacting our emotions before the transformation takes place. Many people have used this method to help cope with their anger, as an alternative to going out and hitting the person with whom they are angry. Taking it out on an inanimate object, such as a cushion, helps some people dissolve the energy of anger, but others argue it can trigger a person to become more violent.

> While you pound the pillow, you are not calming or reducing your anger—you are rehearsing it. If you practice hitting a pillow every day, then the seed of anger in you will grow every day. And someday, when you meet the person who made you angry, you may practice what you have learned. You will just hit the other person and end up in jail. That is why handling your aggression by hitting a pillow, or venting, is not helpful at all. It is dangerous. It is not truly ventilating the energy of anger since anger is not getting out of your system.[12]

When venting, we learn to feel the force of our anger but remain detached from the feelings. If we could pause instead of venting, it would help us connect with our deeper feelings. Pausing will help us to recognize the things that trigger our anger, the things that wind us up. If we slow down, become aware of our feelings, and catch our thoughts, we might not get triggered so easily.

Triggers

If we are to transform our anger, we first have to recognize that we have it, whether as a bottler or a volcano or a bit of both. This recognition can open up the possibility of change, the possibility of doing something different from what we've always done before—whether denying, enacting, or pushing away. Looking at how we do anger, learning what it feels like, will help us work with it more effectively, and more healthily, which will benefit us in the long term, not just in the short term.

As well as getting to know the shape and feel of our anger, it's important to get to know our triggers—the incidents or situations that set us off. By looking in more detail at some common triggers, we can use them as subliminal reminders as we go about our daily lives. We might not identify with any of them right now, but when we are stuck in traffic, or in a supermarket, or at work, we might remember one of these anecdotes and allow ourselves to smile with recognition or even burst out laughing. Even these responses can help us discharge some of the anger.

Road Rage

Over half the Western population spends part of their working day commuting to and from work, and one consequence of this seems to be the phenomenon we label road rage. Those of us who drive a car, motorbike, or bicycle to work will have at least one story about how we have lost our cool. It is even being said that you don't know someone until you've seen them behind the wheel of a car.

The crazy thing is that when we become angry in traffic, we are often putting our own and others' safety at risk. We often become irate because someone has put us at risk, but it is our reaction and our subsequent loss of awareness of our own driving that makes us a danger in our own right. I have seen people jump out of cars in the middle of a busy road and almost end up in a fight, cause an accident, or put their own well-being at risk. I have seen cyclists catch up with the car that almost knocked them over, and thump or kick the door while it is still moving. These are some examples of how anger can set off a chain of events, making a difficult situation a hundred times worse.

On my local main street I once bumped into a friend I hadn't seen for a while. She was walking with a stick. After a few minutes of catching up, she pointed to her right leg. She was wearing an artificial ankle and foot. Shocked, I asked her what happened. She related her story to me: "A truck cut in front of me and then had the audacity to move into the cycle lane, almost pushing me up on the sidewalk. I was so furious that I caught up with it and squeezed up beside it, while it was waiting at the lights. When the light turned green, it turned and its rear end knocked me to the ground, crushing my foot."

The times I have been triggered and put my own life at risk in traffic flashed before me. I too have been knocked off my bike and have been lucky not to end up with a serious injury. I love cycling, and I've tried to teach myself a better way of traveling in busy city traffic. When I'm about to jump a red light, I try to ask myself what the gain is. I'll arrive quicker, I tell myself, but at what cost? It could cost me my life. Is it worth risking being knocked off my bike? This tiny reflection helps me to pause. If I'm stuck in traffic, I tell myself it's a good opportunity to pause, breathe gently, and slow down.

Why do we put ourselves at risk in traffic? I know that when I am riding my bike and a car has almost knocked me off, there is a rush of unpleasant energy diffused through my body. It's so unpleasant I have aversion and want to move away from it. I can hear the words arising in my mind: "You stupid jerk!" When I've identified with these words, I've shouted them out, and have made myself angry. And when I've acted out of the anger, I've tried chasing the car. All this happens in seconds.

Today if I am almost knocked off my bike, I turn toward the unpleasant sensations in the body, and as soon as I can I stop cycling, dismount my bike, and pause on the sidewalk. Sometimes I push my bike along, and get in touch with some sad thoughts. Once they have arisen and ceased, I am able to mount my bike with a calm mind and not think that every driver is now my enemy.

What are you like in traffic?

The Dump

Does any of the following sound familiar? You wake up in the morning feeling out of sorts—well, thinking you feel like shit. You have an argument with someone just before you leave your house, or you leave without saying goodbye.

Either way, without pausing to think, let alone clear it up, you slam the door. You jump into your car seething; anybody who gets in your way is a dumping ground for your frustrated emotions. At the railway station woe betide anyone standing on the wrong side of the escalator. When your train is held up for a few minutes, you start to fume. Arriving at work, you take it out on a colleague or anybody else who slightly messes up. By the time you get home you're so fed up you kick out at the dog, shove the cat out of the way, and round it off with a full-blown argument with your partner. You top that off by having to sleep on the sofa.

It's an unpleasant fact that we often dump our frustrated emotions on people who are close to us, vulnerable, or have less power than us. We can take it out on our children, our partner, the ticket collector, shopkeeper, anyone who happens to be in our way at the wrong time.

Who are the people most likely to get the raw deal in your life? Who do you dump your anger on?

Righteous Anger

Righteous anger gets many of us into trouble, because it is so fueled with what we believe to be our rights. Righteous anger can be strong in some people because they think they are justified in acting out their rage, or they are content to seethe. They believe they are right, otherwise why would they have been sparked off? It's as if we, or the person we believe we are protecting, have been so mistreated that we are totally without blame for our subsequent actions. We are the innocent victims with status. We have a right to be angry. Somebody or something has made us angry. If it wasn't for the incident that triggered us, our lives would be happy and free from conflict.

There are no rights when it comes to acting out destructive behavior. I have found it extremely hard to back down when I think I am 100 percent right. But I've learned the hard way that nobody can hear me when I'm standing tall, screaming, "It's my right!" They are all running away or hiding under the table.

What are you righteous about?

Territorial Anger

People invading our space or taking what we consider to be our space can bring out the worst in us. A thought like "I was here first" is probably our animal instinct coming out. Guarding what we think of as our territory is a basic instinct, but do we want to be driven by it? There are people who erupt if someone has parked in front of their house, gangs fight for control of territory, office workers are outraged when somebody borrows their scissors, and we can even believe a park bench belongs to us.

At work we can also flare up if we think somebody is treading on our toes, taking on work we believe is our sole responsibility. We can even be territorial in our homes, despite the fact that we may have invited in a guest, a friend, or a lover. We live in a world full of territories. And of course wars have broken out over territorial issues.

What are you territorial about? What are you precious about?

Technical Anger

Anger moves with the times. In this computer age, it isn't surprising that a lot of anger gets vented on technology.

I once read a story about a man who put his fist through a television screen because it didn't work. At the time, I thought it was really hilarious. Since then I've resonated with this man. When my computer starts acting up, I've often wanted to throw it to the floor and jump all over it. I never do, but the surge of energy that arises can be frightening.

We have gotten so used to the convenience of high-tech gadgets that when they don't work some people go ballistic. The next time you try to contact somebody who doesn't have voice mail, become aware of what you are feeling. The next time you ring up your phone provider or an airline and you are put on hold, become aware of what you are feeling, and if you miss the feeling, become aware of what you are thinking. The next time you email someone and a week later you still haven't had a response, become aware of what you are telling yourself.

What are the things that frustrate you when they don't perform the way you expect them to?

Some of our triggers have been tagged by the British media "hurry sickness." As one columnist wrote, "People who tap their fingers impatiently as they wait for the microwave to finish or huff and puff while their computer starts up could have the latest malady to modern living—'hurry sickness.'"[13] We live life at such a fast pace that if something does not happen quickly enough, we can become indignant and sometimes enraged.

Let's not forget that we can be triggered by just not looking after ourselves properly. When we don't have enough sleep, or enough food to eat, or when we have the wrong food in our system, or too much food, the slightest thing can trigger us. It's almost as if our defenses are down and any little thing can have us fuming in an instant. So next time you find yourself being sparked off by a trigger, first ask yourself whether you are hungry. Or have you drunk too much coffee? Are you hung over? Or do you need more sleep? This strategy may bring about more harmony in our lives than we could ever imagine.

Watching Our Thoughts

Our external triggers are just part of the picture; what happens inside our own heads is probably more crucial in how we react to a situation. When we take time to pause we begin to see the process, the triggers, and the thoughts that hook us into anger. It can be scary slowing down, and one reason for this is that it can be a shock to hear all the thoughts buzzing around in our heads. We may even be frightened by some of our thoughts when we really stop and listen to them, but be reassured that few of us act out our worst thoughts. Having thoughts is OK—everyone has them—but they don't have to go nineteen to the dozen, and they can be kind and encouraging thoughts instead of the criticisms and put-downs we too often hear: a legacy from our alien, our critical inner voice that I wrote about on page 58. When our thoughts are not punitive, the alien shrinks and the heart and mind surrender to compassionate love.

We need to begin to pay attention to this voice that puts us down. Sometimes the voice speaks so quickly, so habitually, that we're not conscious of it when it speaks, despite the fact that it can have a strong influence on our lives.

If we identify with our thoughts we will start to become them. We will vocalize them to other people in our speech and our actions. When we don't pay attention to the alien, we don't pay attention to ourselves or others. If we tell ourselves we are stupid, worthless, incompetent, we will have no hesitation telling this to others. Watching our thoughts helps us to pay attention to the people we love; it helps to detox our hearts.

Practice: Listening to Our Thoughts

- Pause for a moment and feel your connection with your bed or chair, and the soles of your feet. Become aware of your thoughts. Slow your breath so that you begin to hear your thoughts. Try not to engage with them, just try to be a spectator of your thoughts and listen to what they are saying. For example, if you hear, "Oh, this is a load of old rubbish," let it pass and listen to the next thought, which might be, "I know all this, I just can't be bothered with all this new-age stuff," or "I can't think anymore." Continue to observe the thoughts, whatever they are, particularly noting those that put you down or criticize you. You could write down your putdowns and negative chatter, and see which are the recurring ones.

- Become a spectator of your thoughts again, just watching them arise, change, and cease. If you can catch a positive or constructive thought, write this much bigger on the page. These are the ones we want to encourage.

- Even if you have not caught a positive thought, try either to visualize your negative thoughts shrinking, or write them smaller. When you hear a positive thought, imagine this becoming bigger and bigger in your heart.

- Remember to connect with the breath, and breathe deeply and slowly before moving on to your next activity. 🍃

Redirecting Our Thoughts

As we grow older, life experiences overlie our early conditioning. We may become aware that we are often treated differently according to our gender, sex, race, age, culture, class, sexual orientation, or disability, and that certain privileges are denied to some people. All these can play into feeding our anger at not being seen, heard, or listened to. Life often seems unfair. We've all had disappointments and times when we've struggled to cultivate any happiness. "What's the point?" some of us may think. But this type of thinking—of giving up or having no choice—also feeds the alien in our minds.

We need to work to affirm ourselves, pat ourselves on the back, tell ourselves we have done well to survive the pain we have experienced, let go of our anger, and start to live more fully—in touch with our bodies and our feelings. We need to let go of the putdowns, self-criticism, and blame, and let the alien shrink. One of the ways to do this is to begin to stock up with positive thoughts and self-affirmations.

When we affirm ourselves we cultivate more kindness and gentleness in our hearts. But unless we know our putdowns, we will only skim the surface. When we are aware of our toxic thoughts we can begin to let go of them, and the practice of self-affirmation will have more effect. So when the alien tries to poison our hearts with thoughts like "I'm not worth it" or "It's not worth the trouble," we are still able to hear that positive voice that tells us, "I am worth it" or "It is worth the trouble." The alien thoughts will be nothing but a faint whisper, and our affirmations will constantly reverberate in our hearts.

Once I could only hear "I hate myself." Fifteen years later I can feel and hear the words "I love myself" resonating in my heart and I have begun to identify with this positive voice. Yes, there are days I hear my alien putting me down, and I am continually practicing not identifying with my alien's putdowns. But now I can make a choice as to which voice I listen to or identify with. I am no longer powerless in the grip of my alien, and my toxic thoughts aren't so automatic. Affirming myself has helped me make better choices for myself. I am kinder to my toxic thoughts when they arise. I tell myself I must be feeling vulnerable or hurt so I need to take extra care of myself. My toxic thoughts are a warning that I am at risk of being triggered, at risk of losing my cool, at risk of seething inside. They are the alarm bell telling me I am in touch with some uncomfortable feelings that inform me I could be vulnerable right now. Today when I hear the voice, "I'm not good enough," I pay no attention to it. Yes, I hear it, but I don't believe it, and there is room for a new thought to arise that may tell me how beautiful I am. I don't get attached to that either, I just smile and have gratitude for the positivity arising in the heart/mind.

 ### Practice: An Affirming Practice

Here are a few affirmations for you to consider. Choose one from the list and try saying it five or more times when you wake up and just before you go to bed. Try this for a week and see if you notice any difference. If you do, why don't you continue? If you don't, you can always try something else.

- I am lovable
- I am likeable
- I am good enough
- I matter
- It's OK to face the unpleasant sensations in my gut, neck, or throat that make me sad
- I am responsible for the happiness in my life

Add your own affirmations to the list, and if you are able to say one regularly, your new self-affirming voice will speak to you at the most unexpected moments. Surely it's better to stock up on positive thoughts in your heart than feed your heart with negative chatter? Try to see the practice of affirmations as an opportunity to be kinder to yourself. 🖋

Anger as Fire in Our Hearts

> *Heart is burning, heart is burning*
> *Feel the feelings, feel the feelings*
> *Breathe breathe, breathe breathe*
> *Stop and pause, stop and pause*

"It's not healthy to get rid of your anger. When anger is kept out, pushed away or down, it controls our consciousness," says Atula, a Buddhist psychotherapist. "We must embrace anger, this is where the alchemy is. This is where the transformation can begin."

Anger can protect us, and it can motivate us. Our feelings are part of us, and there is a healthy way of utilizing them. Of course, becoming violent or abusive is not healthy, but luckily this is only one of the ways we can be when in touch with our uncomfortable feelings.

I often use the metaphor of fire to explore anger. It was introduced to me by an organization working with young people: Leap Confronting Conflict. Once one of their trainers, I used to help people explore creative approaches to conflict. In helping people let go of their anger, we help them to see that conflict can have either a destructive or a creative element. Through the following model we examine the causes and consequences of conflict and engage people in finding constructive responses. I have found it a liberating way to help myself and others work with letting go of anger.[14]

Leap breaks down the process of our anger into stages and likens them to the stages of a fire. In a fire we have the fuel, then the spark, then comes the smoldering, then fanning the flames, stoking the fire, and finally the blaze. When used as a metaphor for anger, human beings are the raw material, the lumps of fuel. This recognizes that without our participation there is no conflict. The fire model also states that where there is conflict, there is also the potential for change for the better, and we will look at this alternative response to conflict in chapter 4.

In fire you might find the following stages:

The Fuel	People
The raw material; some is highly combustible; some is damp or flame-resistant.	Wherever people are in contact there is the potential for conflict; this potential will vary according to the degree of combustibility of the individuals.
The Spark	The Incident
Friction causes sparks to fly—some of these sparks land on dry wood, which catches light.	There are always tensions and disagreements between people; some of them cause a spark that ignites conflict.
Smoldering	Brooding
The fuel begins to smolder, the first indication of fire.	Tensions and grievances are smoldering away but unexpressed; the conflict feeds off rumor and gossip.
Fanning	Aggravation
The wind blows and the glowing fuel flickers with flames.	Those who are interested in aggravating the situation provoke it further; thoughts of anger and hurt may be expressed as judgments or hatred.
Stoking	Escalation
The fire consumes the fuel and demands more; huge logs are piled on.	The outside pressures of the social environment intensify the situation; prejudice and disaffection add to the conflict.
The Blaze	Consequences
The fire rages; it becomes a huge blaze and will not easily die down.	People are damaged in a blazing conflict. No one involved is untouched.

Of course some of us don't go through each stage, or the process can be so quick that we quickly flare up and go out. In some families this whole process can take years, in others it can happen in minutes. It is the same in an individual. We'll see in chapter 4 how the stages outlined in this model, instead of leading to a blazing conflict, can be used as opportunities for creative growth. But first let's look at a story that illustrates this (I have changed an urban myth to demonstrate how easily we can set ourselves on fire).

 ## An Urban Myth: Calm the Engine

A man was driving at night when one of his tires burst.

"Damn, it's late and I need to get home!"

He tried to calm himself, but got more and more agitated as he thought about changing his tire.

"Bloody typical," he cried out. "Why does it always happen to me?"

Eventually he got out of his car, opened the back, and scrabbled around for a flashlight. He lugged out the spare tire. Then he realized he needed a jack, but it was missing.

"Shit! Shit! Shit!" he cried, throwing everything on the ground. "I can't even equip myself for emergencies. Some man I am."

When he looked up he saw a light and realized there was a house not far away, so he decided to see if anyone was in. As he walked, he said to himself, "They're not going to answer the door. Even if they've got a jack they're not going to lend it to me. Why should they? They'll be like everyone else, suspicious, bitter, and twisted. Yeah, that's what they are, mean and tightfisted. How am I going to get home? It's all my fault. I'm a failure. Can't do anything right. My dad was right. I'm useless. I'm the laughingstock of Whitstable."

Still ranting inside his head, he walked straight into a door. For a moment he came to his senses and realized he had arrived at the house. He rang the bell, and in a matter of seconds someone opened a window and in a very educated voice called out, "Can I help you?"

The man's anger was triggered and he screamed back, "Keep your bloody posh car jack. What makes you think I want it anyway?"

In a fit of rage he stormed back to his car and tripped over the car jack that he had pulled out of the car without realizing. Cursing, he groaned, "I'm jinxed. Not even God is looking out for me." 🍂

This simple story illustrates some of the deluded thought processes that make us the raw material for fire. Our thoughts are the fuel that causes us to spark, flare up, and catch ablaze. His engine overheated, and his fire needed putting out. Of course most of us would be upset if our tire blew out. But we can see how his assumptions and judgments stirred him into a pitiful rage.

In our urban myth we can see clearly that this man was the fuel, raw and combustible. The faulty tire was the spark that triggered his anger. Instead of acknowledging his upset, perhaps sitting for a moment with his experience of misery and frustration, he begins to beat himself up.

As he walks toward the house he is smoldering so much that he can hear only his deluded thoughts. Unable to pause and hear another point of view from the householder, he is ablaze. Finally he explodes, losing his head. By the time he gets back to the car, he is so angry with himself that he quickly catches light. In the heat of his anger, he doesn't even remember he has a jack. Because he was already fuming, he missed the truth of the situation. This is a lesson to remind us not to attempt anything when we are in a state of anger; we will too often become deluded and duped by our irrational thoughts. He then fans the flames of his anger even more by blaming himself and putting himself down. He stokes his fire further by recalling a belittling comment once made by his father. Again, we often do this toward ourselves, heaping coals on our own heads.

Looking calmly and objectively from the outside, we think if he had only been able to keep calm, his thought process might have been a bit more rational and able to make clearer choices. For example, he could have chosen to try to flag down another car, or call a breakdown organization, or had a more optimistic attitude to getting help from the house.

Digging deeper, we might say that if he were to come into relationship with some of the damaging things his father once said to him, he might improve his low self-esteem so that when this accident happened he might have been able to see it as just one of those chance incidents.

Instead, this poor man was so deluded he didn't even realize that he had picked up his jack and thrown it on the ground. I can resonate with this man. I have been in a similar place, for example when I've mislaid my keys. I have beaten myself up so badly with toxic thoughts for mislaying them that I'm physically unable to find them. The next morning when I look where I've already searched, there they are, staring me in the face. What about you? Do you have a story?

What can we learn about the stoking and fanning of anger from this story?

We can see how anger is often a collection of intoxicating thoughts that we cultivate through our negative thinking. It shows how our rage can have a history, going back to something hurtful someone may have said to us many years ago. The hurt feelings then become corrupted over the years and we beat ourselves up again and again with the same hurtful statement. When we inhabit the unpleasantness of inadequacy or vulnerability, our anger can more easily be sparked, and the layers of our low self-esteem help fuel our anger. The story shows the value of slowing down the internal process and pausing before anger gets worked up into a frenzy and our minds become filled with delusion. But most important, we can see in this story how we create anger in our own heads. We are the fuel, and our blaze is set alight by our thoughts and actions.

There is an Aboriginal saying that we should always look beyond the fire, because if we look into it the flames will send us insane. Our anger can be seen in the same way. If we look into our anger, we will stoke it and become intoxicated by our irrational thoughts. If we can look beyond it, we will start to see something that will help dissolve the energy.

When a driver receives a text and then decides to answer it without stopping, they run the real risk of getting in a collision. They have lost their focus on the road and on other cars passing them on the highway; their attention has been captured by the phone, and within seconds they could be in a wreck.

The same thing happens when attention is captured by a mental state: it becomes isolated, and we lose awareness of the bigger picture. We run the risk of becoming the emotion and acting out on it. For example, I was looking for a new building for an organization that I chair. We moved in, and the landlords did not keep to their agreement to get rid of the bad smell in the building. We chose to move back out because we knew we would lose customers. For a day my attention was captured by the building we had lost. I couldn't think of anything else. Then the next day I began to expand my attention outward and could see we were still fortunate; we were not homeless and could go back to our old rental space. When a deal for the home that one has put one's hopes on falls through, many will be angry and resentful for weeks. This is because they have not looked beyond the house they so much wanted. Contentment lies in awareness of the bigger picture.

Considering Something Different

It is difficult, while we are angry, to get to a place where we can be constructive and make effective changes. Many of us don't get beyond the conflict stage and, if we do, we tend to bottle things up or erupt like a volcano. However, if we know our triggers, hear our thoughts, or become aware of what is happening in our body, we may be able to stop our hearts from becoming full of toxins. The creative element of the conflict is the increasing awareness of the things that create conflict.

Recognizing how anger can often make us passive—in the sense that we react by ranting, complaining, accusing, or by avoiding having to take any action—is creative thinking, and helps us unhook from the toxic thoughts. Knowing all this can help us take advantage of the opportunities that conflict presents. Along with anger comes the potential to do something different. Doing something different might seem risky, because we don't know what the outcome will be. This toxic thinking can prevent us from moving beyond the conflict, and it's likely we'll continue as we've always done. There is a saying, "If you always do what you've always done, you'll always get what you've always gotten. If it's not what you want, do something different."

I remember once asking my therapist why it is always me who has to do the changing. She replied, "If you're happy with the situation, don't do anything; if you're not, you'll have to do something about it." I hated hearing those words, but I knew it was true. I can tell everybody around me that they are the ones who need to change until I am blue in the face, but in the end I am the one who needs to change. I am responsible for all my thoughts and actions. This thinking can be the beginning of detoxing our hearts. In transforming our anger we must become aware of our toxic thoughts.

In the next section we'll look at other ways of doing things, creative strategies for dealing with our feelings of anger and our experience of conflict.

Things to Try

- Watch your thoughts.
- Notice where you feel anger in the body.
- Notice if it feels unpleasant, pleasant, neutral, or a mixture of all three.
- Write down a trigger when you notice it.
- Breathe.
- Say a positive phrase to yourself every day.

4 🍃 Transforming Anger

Many people I know have experienced positive change in their lives after a conflict has developed from a major life crisis—whether a bereavement, a life-threatening experience, or a conflict at work. I'm not suggesting we start creating drama in our lives, I'm just pointing out that conflict can actually bring about positive changes in our lives. Where there is conflict, there are real opportunities for change. There will always be some form of conflict in our lives and this can be a place of transformation. We need to seize these opportunities, rather than lining up for battle.

The Leap Confronting Conflict model shows us how the stages of anger and conflict that we looked at earlier in the fire metaphor can be transformed by positive action and attitudes.

> **People** (the fuel): When people are in contact there is potential for growth; different values, opinions, aims, or expression are the raw material.
>
> **Flash of Insight** (the spark): Examination of the raw issues in a community or a relationship can lead to a flash of insight that brings an issue alive.
>
> **Tentative Response** (the smoldering): The individual looks for areas of shared concern and makes an initial response.
>
> **Encouraged Action** (fanning the flames): Those showing concern for the issue grow in number, encouraging and supporting each other.
>
> **Increased Response** (stoking the fire): Response to the issue increases; the possibility of achievement inspires action from others.

Effective Action (the blaze): Aims are achieved; people celebrate the blazing fire, that beacon that illumines and inspires.

Practice: Slowly Cool Your Fire

- Think of an old conflict and see if you can identify points where you could have brought about positive change. Ask yourself whether you could have done something different. Were there any shared interests? Do you have any insights?

- The next time you are in a conflict, see if you can slow yourself down, and catch yourself in the process of being sparked, smoldering, fanning, or stoking your thoughts. See if you can prevent yourself from going up in a blaze, or withdrawing and silently rumbling away.

Seeing Our Side of Anger

Looking more deeply into this idea of conflict as fire, we see that we ourselves provide the fuel for anger. Not external situations, not other people, but you and I, in our minds and hearts. This early step, and its realization at deeper and deeper levels, is a radical and crucial one. It is a turning point in learning to transform our anger and gradually move away from blaming other people and external circumstances for our reactions.

So what does the fuel break down to? Our personal histories, our conditioning, our judgments, assumptions, stories, and communication are all fuel. By working with these, we can reduce our conflicts. This is not to say that there are no external situations that are unhelpful or difficult, or other people who are unkind or challenging, or situations that are unfair or even unbearable. What I am saying is that we can work differently with our triggers and difficult situations, and see conflict as an opportunity for change. After all, if there is no change the conflict will not cease. Similarly, our internal conflicts are also opportunities for change. Whether we bottle them up or splurge them out, we can still learn from this experience and use it as a potential for change.

It is, in the end, only our own part in any conflict that we can be sure of influencing. Any such work brings us benefit in terms of insight into ourselves, by weakening our unhelpful patterns or broadening our horizons. Such effort is never wasted, even if it doesn't resolve the conflict. One way to learn more about ourselves is to ask questions about our conflicts. What sparked off our anger? What story did we tell ourselves about each person's part in the conflict?

If we look deeper into our experience of anger in this way, we usually find we become angry largely because of our judgments of other people. Sometimes the reasons behind these lie buried deep in our psyche. If we look at a real-life example we can better understand the process. If a friend, someone I really care about, has not called me for a few weeks, I could take this to mean she doesn't care about me anymore. This thought creates friction, it rubs against my heart, fueling my anger. I might then assume she is calling everyone except me. These interpretations then have a domino effect on my thought process and I end up back in my old familiar place of "Nobody loves me. I am unlovable."

Instead of going down this well-trodden path I can transform my anger, see things from a different point of view, and recognize that my interpretations are not accurate but fueled by my conditioning. Stepping back from my anger, I could consider that I haven't called her either, or that her life might be so full that she has no time to talk after a hard day's work.

This is now an opportunity for me to grow from this old place of "nobody loves me" by taking responsibility for my thoughts and interpretations, and recognizing my painful patterns for what they are: patterns, not reality. I could pick up the phone and call her instead of waiting to be called. I used to believe it was my role to be left. I would often push people to end the relationship we were in, so I could hold on to my victim voice: "Nobody loves me, I'm being abandoned."

You could try this reflection to help you slow your process down and get to know your part in a conflict, in order to catch the smoldering fuel before it blazes out of control, or before you stuff all your feelings down onto another layer of festering feelings that have already poisoned your heart.

We all have access to our imagination when we are angry, often with a vivid commentary running through our heads that gives us our own interpretations of others' actions, or by thinking about all the horrible things we want to happen to them, or how they'll be sorry if we show hurt. So connect with your imagination, and use it to your good.

Practice: A Reflection on Our Part in Anger

- Take a deep breath and pause, then read the following and put this book down.

- Close your eyes and take a few minutes to connect with your breath. Allow yourself to feel fully supported, either in bed or on a chair with your feet firmly on the floor. Try to relax your body. Now ask yourself what makes you angry. Choose something small to begin with; it might be something that irritates you or something you want to avoid or which makes you want to withdraw. If you can't think of anything, that's OK, just acknowledge that and continue to breathe. If it's easier, you could ask yourself when you last were irritated, or the last time you experienced some kind of conflict. What was it that sparked that anger? Replay the incident. What happened when you got angry or irritated? Try not to judge; just use your imagination to replay the incident in your mind, without stoking or fanning it to make the incident worse in your mind than it really was.

- What were the triggers? What did you feel? What did you do? Did it flare into a blaze? Did you push it down? What did you gain? What did you lose?

- Ask yourself what else you could have done in that situation. Imagine yourself making different interpretations, acting in a way that could help to put out or prevent the blaze.

- Replay this different way in your imagination, then let it go. As you do so, don't pass judgment, but connect with the breath, becoming aware of your buttocks on the chair and your feet on the floor, or your body lying in bed. Let all the anger drop through to the ground. Then slowly open your eyes.

If you found this exercise difficult, take longer to allow yourself to connect with the breath and become aware of being supported in your chair.

Allow yourself to see the things that spark you off as warnings to alert you to the feelings of vulnerability. We might need to pause when this happens and take a few deep breaths. If we hear our alien fueling our thoughts, we can choose not to listen to it and, most importantly, not to act on those thoughts.

Where there is conflict there is always more than one point of view. If we slow our movie down, and for a few minutes take ourselves out of the leading role, we can begin to see other people and hear their opinions. We also see that we do have a choice; we can act differently when we are triggered.

Time Out of Anger

If we want to detox our hearts of anger and conflict, then we need to keep taking responsibility for ourselves and our part of anger. When we look at anger, perhaps comparing notes with what gets us, or others, irritated or mad, it is obvious there are many things that can spark our rage. A quick introspection should convince us that it is fruitless to try to eliminate the external "causes" of our anger; they are endless and can multiply at alarming speed. We can't control the things that wind us up, or indeed the anger somebody projects onto us, but we can control the way we deal with, respond to, or react to conflict in our lives.

The things that can wind us up are infinite in variety and quantity. I am still learning about my triggers, about what winds me up. For me, this is often a painful memory about childhood, for example, brushing my teeth. I was often clobbered for not cleaning my teeth "properly" as a child. When I see somebody doing it now the way I used to, I automatically start to heat up, ready to blast them as I was blasted.

When we know what winds us up, we have an opportunity to act differently. Here are some of the more common things that can make us angry:

- ourselves—for example, when we mislay things
- a computer when it won't do what we want
- being told a task will take five minutes and it takes twenty
- cancellations and delays

- invasion of our space
- being told we should do this, or that we make someone feel like this
- being bossed around, criticized, or blamed

Do you know what winds you up? If not, make a list now. How many things wind you up? If you think you know, think again. The list is endless. We never know when we'll be triggered or become wound up. All we can do is try to be aware when it happens. Remember, your body will almost always warn you. Knowing some of our common triggers is also helpful. Try to slow down when you see a trigger coming, and give yourself the chance to do something different, because a key step to changing this experience is realizing that we have a choice. The choice is between reacting unconsciously, perhaps from childhood wounds, and responding from a more conscious, positive place. This is the place that does not hook us back into our negative thought patterns. It is the place where we pause rather than react. It is the place where we can have kindness toward ourselves, and awareness of our needs and the needs of others.

So there is always this choice of being present in the energetic or lethargic feelings of anger and taking time out before responding to a situation. This is one of the places where the transformation from conflict into insight can happen. After much investigation of our windups and triggers we will learn that we are the only ones who wind ourselves up or press the buttons. When we allow our minds to be dominated by negative mental states we create our own prisons to live in. Some of them are comfier than others, and we all become a prisoner of our minds. I once heard Thich Nhat Hanh say: "It's not the noise that makes us angry, we make the noise angry." This was a great teaching. It tells us to take time out of what I call "stinking thinking." When I am meditating and my partner is banging around downstairs, I can continue to meditate while fuming about how noisy she is being. Or I could take time out of my meditation, time out of my thinking, and ask her to be quieter downstairs. Or I could choose to sit at another time. When I'm not reacting at all I just see it as noise, which will arise and cease, and that the noise will stop. If I label the noise as banging, I begin to frustrate myself.

Time out is something young people I work with have discovered for themselves. When they are triggered in a session exploring their challenging behavior, they often ask if they can leave the room. They go and sit quietly with their supervisor or talk to them about what is going on for them.

When they return they are calmer and more able to cope, and can explore what was making them angry. By taking action and responsibility around their anger, a transformation has naturally arisen.

My time out has been meditation. Meditating in the morning, I pause before coming into relationship with the rest of the world. On the rare occasions when I don't have time to meditate, I take at least ten minutes to tune in to myself and ask how I am feeling. This act of pausing before launching into my day has allowed me to become aware of my state of mind and heart, and be forewarned before I start communicating. It can unhook me from reacting without any awareness of how I am feeling, and save me from tripping into a whole day of angry or blocked communication or nonverbal communication.

To pause is to slow down our personal movies. When we pause we see the action from different points of view. We don't have to agree with them all, but we can begin to take responsibility for our actions. Instead of saying, "I didn't see it coming," "I can't believe I got so angry," "I just lost it," "I'm never going to speak to that person again," "I'm going to avoid them," or having regret for how we have reacted, we'll have time to find the gap—the creative space in which we can make choices—take action, respond, and choose not to be duped by our negative self-talk. We'll even learn not to blame the triggers themselves, and realize that while an event can upset us it is our own thoughts and stories that get us into trouble.

Practice: A Reflection

- Next time you are triggered or feel wound up, try to notice what is happening (or recall what did happen) in your body. Just breathe, focusing on your breath, or simply count to ten, or walk away from the situation. Any of these will be taking action rather than reacting, and give you a moment to pause.

- You might, however, find you have a resistance to pausing within yourself. If you find you don't want to pause, or after you have paused you still want to follow your negative thoughts, ask yourself why you want to hold on to your anger. Some people enjoy their anger, enjoy the rush, the adrenaline. Others feel that some things must be reacted to no matter what, while others just withdraw. Ask yourself:

  > Am I waiting for an apology?
  > Is it because things seem unfair?
  > Is it because I think I am right?
  > Is it about not wanting to lose face?
  > Is it about my pride?
  > Is it about my rights?
  > Is it to do with discrimination?
  > Do I want revenge?
  > Am I scared?

- Even if you don't want to let go of your anger right now, just by asking yourself "Why not?" you are planting the seed of letting go. To question your actions is a beginning and a big step. Letting go is hard; it involves the loss of an identity that perhaps we have held on to for years, or the loss of coping mechanisms that once helped us. Be gentle in your thoughts. Try not to move into guilt or blame. Thoughts can change; you don't have to act on each one; you can always have another. Be aware of your alien right now. What is it saying? 🍃

A Personal Experience

It might feel that these triggers and our reactions to them are so much part of ourselves that we're just stuck with them. Our alien will often tell us, "I'm always like that. That's just how I am. I'm too old to change." These thoughts may feel just too strong for us to step away from, or perhaps we get some satisfaction by holding on to them or even on to our sense of identity. So I'd like to look in more detail at one of my struggles and how I benefited from tackling it.

One of my biggest triggers has been passport controls and customs. I get wound up half an hour before my plane lands. I've been doing this on a regular basis since the age of nineteen, so I have thirty years of stored anger and resentment every time I see another black person stopped. I've learned the long and hard way that an aggressive attitude just makes going through customs more traumatic. My alien jumps to alert when I'm about to travel: "I always get stopped or hassled!" Although it is often my reality, this just stokes me into an angry attitude so that I'm ready to jump down the throat of anyone who questions me at passport control or customs.

I remember once traveling to a Greek island and having to change in Athens. I had so much attitude when they pulled my passport apart that I blurted out, "Typical! It's always the niggers you pick on. What about all the white people you let waltz through?" The passport controller refused to return my passport. I was taken to a small room and surrounded by guards with guns, and nobody would tell me what was happening. Eventually, fifteen minutes before my plane was due to leave, they handed my passport back. "Enough is enough," I told myself, "I've got to be different. It may be true that I always get stopped because I'm black, but telling them that with attitude just puts me at risk."

My next trip was to America, and I knew I had to be calm whatever happened, as there had been a lot of security hype since September 11, 2001. I reached passport control, and sure enough I was repeatedly asked the same questions. They even wanted to see another piece of photo ID. "Well, I don't drive," I told them politely. "In England I only need my passport when traveling." I had to grit my teeth, but I managed to stay calm and not come out with my usual line, which would inevitably get their backs up. I had learned that, while I thought it was always black people being stopped, other people got stopped too. And even if it was the reality, this negative thought just set me up to become frustrated.

On this occasion I didn't verbalize my thoughts, I just took a few deep breaths. After all, I knew my passport was valid and I had nothing to hide. I even smiled and didn't try to see what he was actually doing to my passport. Connecting with my breath helped me to do something different.

But there was more. The passport controller apologized. I almost fell on the floor! "I'm sorry I questioned you a lot, and gave you a bit of a hard time, but we had an impostor with your exact same name trying to enter the country, so I had to check you thoroughly," he said.

I couldn't believe it! I had never received an apology from passport control for rough or invasive behavior. He even apologized to my white friend when her turn came for her stamp.

Staying calm not only prevented me from losing control, it got me an explanation. If I had been as stroppy as usual, they might have stopped me from entering the country. Recognizing my triggers has definitely paid off. However, I still need to be alert every time I travel. Thoughts of "It's always black people who get stopped" still arise, so I have to be vigilant and remember to pause before my toxic thoughts get me into trouble.

We must be aware how our toxic thoughts can lure us, like bait lures a fish. Perhaps a fish is unable to swim away once it sees the bait, but we can move away when we see our thoughts becoming toxic, and stop telling ourselves unhelpful stories. In the end, we need patience, because our feelings are real, and they can only change with time. Although it may be easier to change what we think, it still can take time.

In an article in the Buddhist magazine *Shambhala Sun*, Pema Chödrön talks about this. "It's said that patience is a way to de-escalate aggression . . . You find yourself in the middle of a hot, noisy, pulsating wanting-to-just-get-even-with-someone frame of mind . . . In order to escape the pain of aggression, you create more aggression and pain. At that point, patience means getting smart: you stop and wait. You also have to shut up, because if you say anything it's going to come out aggressive."[15]

Time out is a smart way to avoid creating more pain and aggression, and buy time for a creative response.

Reaping Consequences

In a well-known Buddhist text, the *Dhammapada*, the Buddha says,

> What we are today comes from our thoughts of yesterday, and our present thoughts build our life of tomorrow: our life is the creation of our mind. If a person speaks or acts with an impure mind, suffering follows them as the wheel of the cart follows the beast that draws the cart.

What we are today comes from our thoughts of yesterday, and our present thoughts build our life of tomorrow: our life is the creation of our mind. If a person speaks or acts with a pure mind, joy follows the person as his own shadow.[16]

If we reflect on the wisdom in this teaching—that, in effect, we contribute to creating our worlds each time we act or react—and apply it to our efforts to free our hearts of anger, we see that we need to work on our minds, and shine a light on our habitual reactions and thoughts. Whoever I work with, young or old, male or female, professionals or client-based therapeutic groups, the phrase "our actions have consequences" strikes a chord in everybody's heart.

In order to stop the same old cycle from repeating and repeating, reaping the same consequences as a result, we have to train ourselves to see things from different points of view. We have to learn not to get hooked into our habitual ways of thinking when things don't seem to be going our way.

Too often it seems easier to believe the old fantasies and negative statements that we come up with when we're angry than to think differently—which would mean letting go of our fixed views and strongly held opinions and beliefs—and change the way we react. It is easier to rush into a familiar place of anger or judgment and toxic thinking, rather than enter an uncomfortable relationship with a host of unfamiliar and scary feelings. When we are angry we are unconsciously dwelling in a place of pain. As Thich Nhat Hanh says, "When a person's speech is full of anger, it is because he or she suffers deeply. Because he has so much suffering, he becomes full of bitterness."[17]

If I look again at my life I can see a sense of progression as I continue to work with my root doubt of thinking I am unlovable. I can see how hard it has been to shift these negative patterns, but how liberating too. Let's take an example. I call a close friend and ask her to attend my birthday party. She tells me she would love to come, but it might be difficult as she is very busy with work at the moment. When she doesn't turn up I have a choice whether to react from a place of anger, or respond from a place of reflection and insight into my feelings. I have a choice about what story I tell myself:

1. If she really loved and cared about me, she would come. If I were special she would come. (I am hurt, but instead of accepting that, I react angrily and flare into my habitual pattern of accusing my friend of not loving me, and concluding that nobody cares about me, nobody loves me.)

2. She might be really busy, but she could at least have come for half an hour. (Although I can begin to see it from her point of view, I've passed a judgment, and my expectation has not been fulfilled. I am left still upset and angry.)

3. Look at all the lovely people who have turned up for me. It's a shame Jeanette couldn't come, but I'm still going to have a good time. (Although I am upset, I have changed my thoughts, and my feelings will also begin to change.)

In these different responses I can see growth: movement toward being less judgmental and more open to others and their needs. The facts remain the same. Jeanette doesn't turn up at my party, but my thoughts have changed and unhooked me from a place of anger, self-blame, and pity. In (3) I acknowledge my upset, but I am not interested in allowing my angry thoughts to be a blight on my enjoyment of the party. I can appreciate all the people who are here for me, and celebrate how I have managed to liberate myself from an old thought pattern: that nobody cares about me. I can hold on to the affirmation and nourishment my friends have given me at my party, and I can also accept that something is going on in my friend's life that has made it difficult for her to attend.

Of course, it's not easy to have such clarity when we are in a conflict. The thoughts arise so quickly that we can often find ourselves stuck at (1) with the situation escalating, so we all too easily end up dwelling in this state of anger and end up being a victim. As Ayya Khema so skillfully points out, "Anger and our craving to be loved are two sides of the same coin. In each case we have the same underlying difficulty. If someone hurts us, it may express their lack of love, or it could be because they didn't feel well or even that they just don't know how to deal with people. To us, however, their conduct comes across as rejection. If we want love but are not shown any, we will grow sad and then angry."[18]

The truth is that when we spiral down into our habitual patterns of low self-esteem, we can hear only ourselves; we get lost in old, stagnant griefs and beliefs. This is when we can get firmly stuck at stage (1), believing our friend doesn't care about us. Then the stoking and the fanning of the flames can begin. Once we're in this position, we'll try to find ways to confirm this fixed view, dredging up all the things that our friend has done to us—or we imagine she has done to us—in the past, and which we have resented. The fire has begun to rage in our hearts.

I have wasted hours on many past birthdays lamenting the friends who didn't turn up, while not enjoying all those who did. Our thoughts have consequences; they can shape a life of misery or a life of joy. The mini-insight is that if we can acknowledge that we are upset, we can perhaps stay in the present and hear what others are telling us or see what is really happening.

The next time you become irritated, upset, or angry, try to catch your thought process. It will happen very fast to begin with, but eventually you can follow the thoughts as they pop up. By hearing what is going on inside your head, you can stop yourself from falling down the same hole again and again. Or even if you fall down the same hole a few more times, at least you have paid attention to it, and eventually you will be able to walk around it without toppling in. You might even be able to hear some positive and constructive thoughts amid all the negative chatter and be able to respond creatively by choosing to do something different.

Letting Go

What if it is too late for pausing or catching our thoughts? What if we are already on fire? Even if the blaze of our anger is already raging, internally or externally, if we can begin to let go of negative thoughts that add fuel to the fire, and stop stoking, it will die down. The conflict in our lives will then become easier to manage.

When we transform our anger, we transform ourselves. Where there is change, there is always something that has to be let go, as well as something to embrace. When transforming the energy of our anger, it is our pain, our views, our judgments, or our blame that we need to let go.

When you begin to investigate, you notice, for one thing, that whenever there is pain of any kind—the pain of aggression, grieving, loss, irritation, resentment, jealousy, indigestion, physical pain—if you really look into that, you can find for yourself that behind the pain there is always something we are attached to. There is always something we're holding on to . . . And then you have a choice; you can let go of it, which basically means you connect with the softness behind all that hardness.[19]

Admittedly, letting go is never as easy as it sounds, because of our attachment to our pain in the form of a fixed view that we can never change. But if we can let go—of our views, stories, anger, and old identities—we begin to cultivate much more happiness and harmony in our lives.

It is important to recognize that we can begin to let go without understanding why we experience feelings of anger or why we might have negative thoughts whirling around in our heads. Wanting to know why can just keep us stuck. We just have to acknowledge that there is anger in our hearts, then the process of letting go can begin. Letting go makes room for something new to arise in our hearts.

Remember that this is the beginning of letting go of our anger. It's a process, and the anger won't disappear overnight. There will be days when everything seems to go wrong, and we will be triggered, and there will be days when the sparks fly right over our heads, hardly disturbing our thoughts.

Some people use visualization to help them let go of their anger. They visualize their anger as something physically powerful, such as an ocean wave, a thunderstorm, or water extinguishing a blaze. Visualizing our anger on this metaphorical level is a safe way to explore it without adding more fuel. We can imagine ourselves letting go, using the visualization to become aware of our anger, and, in our imagination, let it rise and fall away naturally.

If you are a visual person, try to find your own image of anger, one with some kind of crescendo but a calm ending. Stay with the energy as it surges then ebbs away. If visualization is difficult, turn back to the list of affirmations and practice affirming yourself. Affirmations can help quiet the negative chatter that stokes our thoughts.

We need to be realistic about what we can cope with. Try not to set yourself up to fail. Think in terms of small steps, of moving slowly and skillfully. It's OK to say, "I can't face this conflict right now," or "Today I can't be in the same room as X." Hopefully, after pausing and taking time out, you'll feel more able to face the situation another time. Ayya Khema writes:

> If we accept that sometimes we cannot overcome our anger and resentment, and that we are only harming ourselves, we can at least take our mind off it until the negativity has subsided a little, or the situation has changed sufficiently for us to be able to practice loving-kindness and compassion again.[20]

Walking away or admitting to ourselves that we can't cope with a situation at this moment is not losing face, or a crying shame—it means looking after ourselves. It means we have temporarily lost connection with the other person, and we need to reconnect with kindness when we are in a better place. Correction before connection is a recipe for disaster.

Effective Action

Choosing Constructive Action

It is clear from many different religions that, even thousands of years ago, mental states such as anger were seen as emotions that human beings had to work with. Christianity, Judaism, Hinduism, Buddhism, and other religions all have their written discourses on how to transform anger. These teachings range from loving thy neighbor to cultivating compassion and mindfulness. These teachings all point to ways in which we can change our conditioned reactions for more creative responses.

All the world's major religions emphasize the importance of love, compassion, and tolerance. Through my own personal journey of meditation I am still learning how the cultivation of loving-kindness, compassion, joy, and peace can help me to conquer the anger, hatred, and fear within my heart. But all too often we don't know how to be creative with our anger, or how to cultivate the more positive emotions that might put out the anger in our hearts. The Buddha has said, "He who can control his rising anger as a coachman controls his carriage at full speed, this man I call a good driver: others merely hold the reins."[21]

I was once sitting with a group of anger management trainers exploring the ways we deal with our anger. We each created our own list, and found ourselves asking whether even half the things we do to help control our anger are helpful. I asked if I could share this with my readers, and they agreed. Here is our list.

- having a cigarette
- breathing deeply
- having a drink
- eating
- having a bitch session
- counting to ten
- screaming
- taking it out on others
- meditating
- having sex
- shouting
- slamming the door
- putting on really loud music
- phoning a therapist
- talking to someone
- punching something
- stomping around
- crying

Read the list again, circle which things you do, and add to the list. Ask yourself how beneficial are the ways you work with your anger. Try not to make a judgment about the ways in which you cope; just ask yourself what you have gained from responding or reacting in this way, and what it has cost you. Remember we all have ways of coping with difficult feelings, no matter how destructive, and they have served us in the short term.

Now here is another list of things that people have tried, with an emphasis on working constructively with their anger and channeling the energy.

- writing a letter of complaint
- writing protest poetry
- becoming an artist
- campaigning
- signing a petition
- picketing
- striking
- lobbying
- demonstrating
- holding a vigil
- boycotting
- taking one's business elsewhere

Of course none of these strategies guarantees a conflict-free resolution to the situation that triggered anger in the first place, but they do allow the surging energy to be redirected into more constructive expression. What is different from the first list is that all the ways cited here face the anger and then channel it. In the first list there were many instances of feelings being suppressed, stuffed back down using food, drink, sex, etc. These methods can work in the short term, but the angry feelings have not been dealt with. The second list also introduces some types of ritual to help us deal with our anger.

I have often thought of writing a letter of complaint when I've been outraged about something, but then wondered what was the point. Then one day I returned from a holiday and complained to a friend about how insensitive an airline had been about serving me meat when I had clearly ordered a vegetarian meal. One of the air stewards made a joke about it, and found it amusing that I had almost eaten meat.

My friend said, "Why don't you write and complain?" I did, and to my surprise I received a letter two months later with a travel voucher for a hundred pounds and an apology.

Similarly, when I receive an email campaign, I delete it because I think, "Oh, what's the use, who cares about my opinion?" But I've realized that it can have an effect. The UK Burma campaign for human rights and democracy in Burma has launched several email campaigns asking people to sign up and forward messages to multinationals who are investing in Burma. These email campaigns have persuaded a number of tour operators and well-known British companies to withdraw their investments. Not every email campaign is successful, of course, but at least our voice is heard, and someone probably loses sleep over it.

Some people prefer to turn to meditation, prayer, or chanting in times of conflict as this helps to still their turbulent energy and cultivate a more peaceful state of mind. Others enroll on courses to explore their anger, or put themselves in therapy. These ideas might seem a little daunting. Many of us live such busy lives and have little time to catch up with friends, let alone take time to write a letter or go on a course. How many of us have time to set up a campaign, or the ability to pay for therapy, or time to meditate? But the reality is that if we want change we will have to make some space for it.

 ### Practice: Planning Change

- Just pause for a moment and try to think of ways you could deal with issues you feel strongly about.

- Perhaps make a list of things you could do.

- Even if you never do any of them, this might give you the satisfaction of knowing that you could if you wanted to.

- In a year or two you might actually find yourself trying some of the things you identified.

Anger can be turned into an important catalyst for altruistic deeds. Freedom fighters like Nelson Mandela and Martin Luther King, and pioneers like Mary Seacole and Mary Wollstonecraft, have exemplified this through their actions of campaigning and tending to the needs of the oppressed and the wounded. We could say that people like Mandela dissolved anger by acting beyond their ego for the sake of humanity.

Some of us choose our jobs because of injustices done to us as children. Our choice of career can help channel and transform the anger we have stored and collected. I know for myself that as a child I was not listened to, and decisions were made that nearly cost me my life. I survived, but my unconscious anger pushed me into becoming a journalist and writing about communities of people who didn't have a voice in the mainstream. I could campaign and fight for their rights. I covered black deaths in custody, and land rights in Australia, and wrote stories about Nicaragua, black South Africa, black Europeans, feminism, and the injustices suffered by black people in Britain. It was also no coincidence that I became a trainer in anger management and conflict resolution.

Through my current work as a trainer I believe I can correct some of these injustices, exploring what is behind the destructive actions, rather than trying to silence them through sedation, exclusion, sectioning, or imprisonment.

Lillie Stoute, a fellow trainer in anger management, says, "My anger is precious. It is one of the things that helps me get up in the morning and face the world as a black woman. It makes me get up and fight for justice. It is what helped me attend a meeting at my daughter's university and discuss the issue of racism around a table of bigwigs. I love my anger. Anger doesn't have to be negative." She believes that anger is one of the things that make people go out and vote, protest against war, fight for rights, and get unfair decisions overturned, and that helps parents get their children into a decent school. And some of us make a career out of our anger. One of my junior school reports read: "Valerie Mason-John is the defender of the underdog." I have to be aware that I'm defending from a place of compassion and not a place of anger.

Compassion as an Antidote

I remember once being on retreat and asking my spiritual heart surgeon what compassion was, to which she replied, "You'll only know what compassion is when you begin to feel it toward yourself."

I left that meditation interview confused and angry. I caught myself becoming angry toward her, so I tried to stay with my feelings rather than give my anger more life by blaming her for not giving me the answer I wanted.

I later became aware that I was holding back tears. I recognized this feeling: it was a familiar excruciatingly painful knot in my throat, a plug that stopped my tears from surfacing, and prevented me from crying.

What if I just let the tears come, I asked myself, and allowed myself to cry? How would that be? In that moment I began to understand compassion. I remembered something I had read about compassion: "Compassion is when kindness meets suffering."

Could I be kind to my pain, my suffering? I knew then I had to start being kinder toward myself if I was to continue to grow and develop, otherwise that knot in my throat might one day choke me to death. Since that day I have allowed my tears to flow. Sometimes it's just a trickle, sometimes they come from a deep place, but they do dry up and stop.

Some months later, I realized compassion toward myself meant being kind to myself every time I messed up. Instead of beating myself up using my alien, toxic thoughts, and putdowns every time I did something unskillful or when I didn't keep to the pact I'd made with myself, I visualized picking myself up, giving myself a hug, and saying to myself, "You poor thing. You must be vulnerable, sad, and frightened."

My anger would dissolve, and I would no longer be at risk of lapsing into my unhealthy habits of overeating or self-hatred. Tomorrow has become a brighter day.

Compassion is perhaps the most powerful antidote to anger. Compassion can transform not only our blaze, but the blaze in another person too.

When we are compassionate with ourselves we stop giving ourselves a hard time, stop punishing ourselves, and accept that anger has arisen, and we don't have to act it out. We also become compassionate to others. When we are compassionate to ourselves, people often see this and can't help being kinder to us as well. Compassion allows us to see that, while we are in pain, the person we are in conflict with is in pain too. Compassion helps us realize that nobody really wants to suffer.

A prerequisite to compassion for another person is to see things from their point of view, to empathize with them. When we are open to seeing and hearing the other person's point of view we can acknowledge that when we are in pain, the stranger sitting next to us who drops all their litter might be in pain too.

We have no idea what people are carrying in their hearts as they walk along the street. Someone who pushes us out of the way might be in a rush because they've received some bad news. Someone who speaks harshly to us might be terminally ill. The driver who cuts in front of us might have learned of a crisis. If we could remember this the next time we feel vulnerable, or when someone speaks harshly to us, or is inconsiderate, we might be able to respond with compassion, rather than react and add fuel to the fire. Whether or not this is the case, the act of empathy itself will change us and can transform the whole situation.

However, to be compassionate does not mean you have to be submissive, nor does it mean that people never do unskillful things that we find painful. In reality there is unskillfulness all around us. Being compassionate means taking action. It means opening up our hearts without being taken advantage of or abused. Compassion means standing up for ourselves while not abusing others. It means recognizing our needs and the needs of others. When we state our needs, we are being compassionate toward ourselves. When we don't state what we need, people can abuse our kindness and understanding.

A traditional story illustrates this. There was once a swami who lived in a temple. After some months a cobra moved into his courtyard. The swami became concerned because the cobra was biting his visitors, so they stopped visiting him. The swami decided to try to persuade the snake not to bite his visitors because they were coming for good reasons. The snake eventually agreed, and gradually his visitors filled the temple again. The swami was so pleased that he decided to look for the cobra and thank her. He was shocked when he found the cobra. She was ill and had many wounds. The cobra had gone from being a happy snake to being sad, hopeless, and miserable.

"What has happened to you?" asked the swami.

"Nobody is scared of me since I've stopped biting," she explained. "The children throw stones at me and drag me around by my tail."

The swami was aghast. "I know I asked you to stop biting my visitors but I didn't tell you to stop hissing."

Letting go of our anger does not mean we must stop protecting ourselves. Letting go of our anger means recognizing it so that we can transform it through constructive action and compassion.

Nourishing Ourselves

When we take positive action and respond creatively to our anger, we are taking good care of ourselves. Taking care of our hearts, minds, and bodies is taking positive action. Learning to be kind and loving toward ourselves is a challenge. It is also part of the lifelong practice of working with our anger.

There is a meditation called the *metta bhavana*, which has its origins in the Buddhist tradition. *Metta* means loving-kindness, and *bhavana* means to develop. This meditation teaches us to be kind and gentle by cultivating a positive relationship with ourselves and the rest of the world. Loving-kindness can be the beginning of compassion for ourselves and the way to end anger in our hearts and minds. It is what I have used to begin releasing the toxins of anger, hatred, and fear from my heart. It has been the alchemy in my life.

The first stage of this meditation turned my life around. It was here that I faced the question, "If I can't feel love for myself, how can I feel healthy love for others?"

Below are instructions for this first stage of the meditation. (Some of the other stages will be used in other sections.) I hope you find it as revolutionary, over time, as I did.

 Practice: Developing Kindness toward Yourself—
A Metta Practice

- Close your eyes, grounding yourself on your seat. Make sure you are fully supported and your feet are placed firmly on the ground.

- Become aware of the breath permeating your body. Imagine it to be a spray clearing the toxins from your heart.

- After a minute try to visualize looking back at yourself, or see yourself in a beautiful place that you enjoy. Or just silently call your name. Remember to breathe.

- After another minute say to yourself, "May I be happy," then breathe and acknowledge how this feels. Then say, "May I be well," then breathe and acknowledge how this feels. Then say, "May I be kind toward my suffering," then breathe.

- Allow yourself to sit in stillness with whatever arises. After a few minutes say, "May I cultivate more kindness within my heart. May I cultivate more peace within my heart. May I continue to develop and grow."

- Continue to recite these phrases, leaving a minute or two between each, staying connected with yourself all the time.

- After ten minutes bring the practice to an end.

If you practice this weekly it will begin to transform your heart. If you do it daily it will bring about positive change in your life.

If our hearts are full of love and kindness for ourselves, there is little room for anger. Such mental states might arise, but love is the cleansing water that puts out the flames of anger.

I hope this section has shown that anger is best not buried, repressed, or unthinkingly acted on; it is not our enemy. Where there is anger, there is the potential for wisdom. Where there is wisdom there is room for change. Facing our anger is wisdom.

Things to Try

- Acknowledge the anger in your heart
- Recognize that conflict can be an opportunity for change
- Learn to slow down and pause
- Use the breath
- Be aware of your feelings
- Be aware of fanning and stoking your thoughts

- Be aware of your interpretations and judgments
- Catch the putdowns
- Affirm yourself
- Learn your common triggers
- Know your thoughts—let go of your thoughts
- Recognize there are more points of view than your own
- Take time out
- Meditate
- Visualize letting go of your anger
- Cultivate more kindness and compassion
- Develop loving-kindness toward yourself

5 Uncoiling the Guises of Hatred

A Fable

And the mind spoke, saying, "Tell me about my hatred."

The heart said, "Your hatred is your inability to wholeheartedly love or forgive yourself. Without true compassion or love for yourself, there will always be a flicker of hatred in your thoughts. Your hatred has its roots in your suffering, in your wounded self. Whatever it is that has hurt you, or whoever has not given you what you desire, you have shut out of your life. Your hatred is the layers of frustrated anger that have piled up inside your heart from the moment you were born. In your hatred your mind is unable to see or listen to anybody else's point of view. It is full of ill will. Anger laced with ill will is hatred. Your hatred wants to annihilate anything that contradicts you or gets in your way. Your hatred is aversion to feeling sensations in the body. And when you move away from your feelings, you become separate and other from whatever the trigger was. Your hatred is the polarization of us and them, of I and you, of "I'm right" and "you are wrong." At its worst it is the acting out of your most terrible thoughts. This is your hatred. It is the complete denial of your heart. Your heart has been pushed out of your mind. 🌿

My Story: Recognizing Hatred

Hatred has been a part of my life. I have had to learn what hatred feels like inside, living with an alien—the critical voice in my head—whirling around in my head to the refrain, "I hate myself." I was shocked the first time I actually heard this voice. I remember clearly where I was, standing on a platform waiting for a train, my fists clenched and my body rigid, and the alien in my head shouting "I hate myself" over and over again with such pace and venom.

I had begun to slow down my life, and this was when I began to hear the toxic thoughts spinning around in my heart and my head. I also became aware of the tension I was constantly holding on to. My jaw and face was often tight with fear, and my stomach was so clenched that it often rejected what I put into it. I also started to realize that the alien was strongest when feelings of vulnerability surged through my body. I hated feeling vulnerable; it made me think I was unsafe, dirty, and powerless.

Hating myself was a way of pushing out the scary feelings that made me feel so nasty inside. My alien was like a friend who kept at bay the feelings I didn't want to experience. But in hating myself I had become alienated from most of my feelings, apart from the overwhelming highs and lows.

Once I became aware of this critical voice, I began to shout back, "I love you!" For several years I battled with the alien in my heart, but just saying "I love you" every time I heard it wasn't enough. I had to learn to stay with the vulnerable feelings when they surged through me. Once I was able to stay with the stormy feelings, they became gentle waves. I began to experience a whole new range of emotions between the highs and lows, and realized that I could wake up with pangs of sadness, and in a few hours' time have pangs of happiness, excitement, or boredom, and by the end of the day I could be experiencing something completely different. My body had begun to relax, slowly letting go of the toxic tension. Then "I hate myself" gradually became a whisper, and "I love myself" slowly became one of my heart's echoes.

I had to look inside my heart and take responsibility for my happiness and my suffering. I had to recognize I was my own worst enemy, and that I even made the people I loved my enemies. People I'm irritated or angry with just become enemies of my mind. Whenever they appear in my thoughts I lose all peace of mind, because narratives about what I'm going to say or what I will do set off whirring around in my head. These unhelpful dramas are a signal that I need to detox my heart and let go of the smoldering frustration and pain deep inside me. My self-hatred has been diluted by the practice of self-metta, and I had to learn to forgive and let go of the pain from my past. Working with my self-hatred is challenging, because much of it has arisen from the injustices in my life, and they require forgiveness.

When I look back at my personal story I can see how the layers of frustration piled up in my heart and became self-hatred. Of course I wasn't born with self-hatred; those feelings of rage for myself began in childhood. I couldn't tell you how many people parented me, or even how many people sexually abused me, but I know it's more than I can remember.

Part of my process for moving away from hatred was an adaptation of the traditional loving-kindness meditation I introduced in chapter 4. This was something I practiced daily for almost a year. I will introduce it later in the chapter as a tool you can use to uncoil any hatred in your heart. I still practice this meditation regularly. Today I hear a friendly voice within saying "I love myself." I still hear "I hate myself" from time to time, but the love in my heart has helped to calm it down. This calm has helped me to see that what I am hating is the young child who was unable to protect herself. The calm has shown me that I don't hate all of myself, and that I need to make peace with the vulnerable child who was once helpless. And when the voice of the alien arises, I tell it, "It's not true, it is just an old habit." This kind loving voice will only continue to whisper sweet words in my heart if I pay attention to myself. I also realized that my self-hatred was part of the hatred I put out there in the world. When I change, everything around me changes, and I look at the world through different eyes.

The liberation from this self-deprecating voice emerges when we can see clearly there is no self to hate. No self to love either. Just an unfolding of conditions and thoughts that have nothing to attach to. When we start beating ourselves up we are attached to a past. Acceptance is in this moment now. Peace arises when we can set ourselves free from the proliferation of thinking. The thinking creates identity and we begin to believe these fictions as if they were fact. The thoughts like "I'm no good; I'm a loser" may still float into our psyche, and they will have nothing to attach to if we don't identify with the thoughts. If we don't think the thoughts.

I realize that I had taken the notion that what goes up must come down and applied it to the teaching of allowing thoughts to arise and cease. Unconsciously I had accepted that my thoughts would rise up and fall back down into my being. Now I see more clearly that this teaching is telling us that thoughts will rise and end. Buy a bottle of bubbles, and blow into the stick, and see the bubble rise—and at some point it ceases into emptiness. Our thoughts can be like that too. You may experience them as strong, weighty, alluring, exciting, and all-consuming, but left alone they will pop into nothingness.

One day we will see that when an unpleasant feeling arises in the body there is no need to react at all with the phrases that have become our life sentences—"I'm unlovable" or "I hate myself." We breathe deeply into the discomfort and allow the sensations to dissolve without having to react at all. This is freedom from the prison of our minds, freedom from the misery we keep on creating whenever we react to sensations with reactive thoughts.

Seeing the Hidden

Hatred is such a strong emotion that few of us are willing to admit we experience it. We might see it as something that happens "out there" and beyond our control, because we believe, or want to believe, we are not capable of hatred. And it's probably true that most of us won't experience the intense, sustained hatred that actually leads to violence and destruction.

But for most of us there will be times when we experience some of the toxins of hatred through jealousy, rejection, or abandonment, or perhaps in a fleeting moment of rage when our lives are put at risk through carelessness or threatening behavior. On whatever scale it is experienced, hatred is war in our hearts. If freedom of heart is a mind and heart in balanced and peaceful union, hatred is the exact opposite. Hatred is toxic. It poisons our hearts and minds, pushing out the love from our hearts, threatening the positive in our relationships with people, and slowly destroying us. Hateful thoughts become so intoxicating that they distort the mind. At full strength they can cause us to harm ourselves and others through our thoughts, words, or actions.

Although anger is the fuel for hatred, hatred is not necessarily the outcome of anger. We can be angry, or have angry thoughts, but not bear grudges, ill will, or want revenge. But if we continue to carry the anger in our hearts for long periods of time, these feelings can fester and turn to hatred. The Dalai Lama advises us that when anger arises, we need to make sure it doesn't culminate in full-blown hatred.

Although few of us will direct this full-blown hatred toward others, we will probably experience anger, dislike, ill will, prejudice, desire for revenge, or envy, because most of us make a choice not to act out the potent fantasies that can obsess our thoughts. However, these toxins will pollute our hearts. Toxins of the heart are layers of frustration that accumulate as we grow up, and these can manifest verbally in expressions such as "I don't want to talk about it," "I'm disappointed in you/ me," "No, I'm not mad, just annoyed and irritated," "I can never trust you again." Or we shut people out of our lives altogether. Yet we poison our hearts when we are unable to feel love, kindness, or compassion toward whatever we are blocking out or running away from. This avoidance may calm our thoughts in the short term, but if we refuse to come into relationship with our fear or hatred in the longer term, if only within ourselves, we are allowing it space to grow.

Alternatively we can stoke up our ill will, much as we do with anger (as we saw in the story of calming the engine, and the Leap model of anger as fire). The blaze, where anger is out of control, is hatred; but before we get to the blaze there are the logs we throw onto the fire to build it up. These logs are our thoughts. We can move from thinking, for example, "She/he really gets on my nerves," to "I really don't like that person," and then to "I can't stand the sight of that person," so quickly that we hardly notice it.

The Different Faces of Hatred

Actions

What does hatred look like? As with anger, we can react in various toxic ways to hatred. We can see hatred spoiling our hearts when we are:

- argumentative
- uncooperative
- disruptive
- dismissive

- judgmental
- complaining
- resentful
- withdrawn
- silent
- unforgiving

Although these might seem appropriate when someone hurts us, we must begin to realize that this way of reacting to conflict is the cultivation of subtle toxins of hatred that take root in our hearts. Sooner or later we will need to detox our hearts.

During a fifteen-week anger management program that I deliver (designed by Theresa Holman on behalf of Clean Break), the participants explore their continuum of anger toward hatred. They learn that their anger can become hatred, and that it can be acted out externally through aggression, or internally through depression.[22]

Aggressive Types
- voice becomes louder
- shouts, swears
- stutters, agitated, argues
- racing heart, waves arms
- stomps, smashes things
- kicks doors
- pushes, slaps
- hits out, fights
- assaults others
- uses weapons
- commits manslaughter
- commits murder
- gets killed

Depressive Types

- talks to oneself
- mutters, can't eat, sickness
- has headaches, nausea
- can't breathe
- won't get up
- won't go out
- remains alone, isolated
- uses drugs, alcohol
- has eating problems
- has anxiety, asthma
- cuts or burns oneself
- takes an overdose
- commits suicide

Although some of the above behavior might come across as extreme, there are some things on this list that most of us can identify with. If there is hatred in our hearts it will have an effect on our whole being, physically, mentally, and spiritually. Our minds will corrupt anything to do with loving-kindness, compassion, joy, and peace.

Body Language

As with anger, our body language can help us identify our emotions, but in this case we might notice our body language is aggressive when we are faced with somebody. Our body language can show quite blatantly that we don't want to be in the same room as that person, even if we are not consciously aware of it. We might avoid eye contact, look beyond or through them, try to make the person invisible, or leave the room. With stronger feelings of unpleasantness our body language is often more violent. We become aggressive in the way we move around the person we don't like, for example, by waving our hands in his or her face, and sometimes this can be quite threatening.

While running workshops for adults on exploring and shifting their negative emotions through movement, voice, and play, I have discovered how common it is to find a whole host of feelings, such as vulnerability, bubbling beneath the hatred. I find again and again that behind the hatred is deep-seated fear and pain. Strange as it may sound, anger and hatred can be easier to welcome than grief, sadness, and hurt. By focusing on our anger we can think we are in control and conceal our pain from ourselves. Anger and hatred seem to have more energy. When we experience emotions of grief and sadness it can weigh us down, and immobilize us. I professionally train schoolteachers, and they will tell me it's far easier to get angry with their students when they experience sadness and hurt. The anger moves them away from emotions that would make them feel vulnerable in front of a class.

The first step in working with these emotions in a workshop setting is to create a space in which each participant can start to come into relationship with their blocked emotions. We then explore together what anger, chaos, playfulness, and stillness feel like in the body, what they sound like, how they move. The rules of no hitting, no throwing, and no touching are designed to create a safe space. When I lead a group through anger, it is full of fire and energy, but when I take the group through the journey of chaos, the place where much hatred can be manifested, the movements become heavy, strange, and repetitive. This is a place where people can get stuck, and this is often acted out through repetitive movements.

Some people are able to create wonderful things out of chaos, while others fear what it can bring, because they can lose control when they experience anger. Periods of play and stillness always follow the chaos section of the workshop as a necessary stage in recuperation and reflection. I encourage people to name their emotions. I understand that stating you are in touch with sadness, hurt, or grief may make you vulnerable. But you could just say, "It's not working for me right now." Or, "I need some help right now to deal with the situation." I've done exactly this while working with groups of thirty or more youth. And it's inspiring what happens. I get to pause, the young people get to pause, and I don't end up shouting at them or expressing my anger and frustration.

Some reflection after completing some of the practices in this chapter, before plunging back into the busyness of life, may also be helpful. Whenever we are faced with strong emotions we need to look after ourselves.

The Different Notes of Hatred

Our hatred has a range of components, like the notes on a piano. The scale of hatred is made up of thoughts, interpretations, and judgments as its notes. When I was a child, one of the places I used to escape to when I was angry was the piano. I took great delight in thumping the keys and letting out my frustration. There was never just one note sufficient to express the music of my frustration; there were many notes, high and low, with different chords all mixed up together. I tend to think of hatred as being a bit like this, many different toxic notes making up the scale of hatred.

Dislike: To dislike is to have thoughts of aversion toward somebody or something. In its most extreme form it becomes aversion, a total repugnance. Aversion is hatred; it has the taint of both anger and ill will. We may dislike somebody because they irritate us, or because they don't live up to our perhaps unconscious expectations. When our dislike takes a grip on our hearts it can manifest as aversion. One way we begin to deal with this is by completely avoiding what we dislike, doing our utmost to keep it out of our lives.

Ill will: When hatred poisons our hearts, there is always an element of ill will—antagonistic and hostile feelings. It is as if we have been wronged by somebody. This may be real or it may be just the conjuring of our thoughts, or a mixture of both. We become so irritated that we can't let go of the feeling. We get hooked into how mistreated we have been, and mull over what we will do or say to the person we believe has treated us, or someone else, unfairly. When ill will poisons our hearts, there is not much joy left in our lives.

Ill will can be all-consuming. It fuels hatred, and can be triggered by a variety of things: criticism (whether justified or not), loss (of belongings, status, or a person), betrayal, disappointment, etc. Ill will is insidious; before we know it, we are obsessed; all we can think of is proving that the other person is wrong, and making things the way we want them.

The feature that distinguishes anger from hatred is the absence or presence of ill will. Revenge and resentment are components of ill will. When we are overwhelmed by this toxin we can resent whatever caused our suffering, and sometimes we will seek revenge. Retaliation is common among young people, and in gangs. It is often the essence of war or crimes of passion.

We could say that the incidents of September 11, 2001, were fueled by ill will and revenge. Some people claim Osama Bin Laden and his confidants plotted their attack on America in apparent retaliation and revenge for American policies since the 1940s. In revenge, America and Britain declared a war on terrorism and invaded Iraq. Many wars have begun like this. Of course there are more complicated reasons why wars break out, but the essence is that hatred breeds more hatred.

When we harbor resentment in our hearts, we are unwilling and unable to let go of the perceived injustice, unable to forgive or come into discussion with what is making us angry. Holding on to our hurt, then, can be a way of composting our hatred. It provides the fertile soil in which resentment will begin to sprout inside our hearts. I've met many people who've had a difficult encounter with a colleague, friend, or lover, and years later their hearts are still seething.

Envy and jealousy: These two belong to the same family. Envy can creep into our hearts when we want what another person has. It's all about gaining what we don't have. What others have seems better, and we fantasize about having it, even if it means taking it away from them. Envy is also aroused by the resentment of the good fortune of others. We can be envious of people in a better house than ours, or envious of their success. This toxin is particularly damaging as it deprives us of the natural response of sympathetic joy for another's good fortune. Envious people never seem to be satisfied with their lot. We might think:

- Why was s/he promoted and not me?
- It's about time they noticed me and stopped giving all the attention to my sister
- It's not fair; I want to live where it's warm too
- S/he always gets the best presents

When we are jealous we often become suspicious or fearful of being replaced—by a newborn sibling, a colleague at work, another person in a friendship or relationship. This fear of replacement can throw us into chaos. Jealousy is often spurred by the fear of losing something—for example, fear of losing our partner to someone else. We become jealous of our partner's every interaction with others. We may also have strong thoughts of:

- I want to be the only one
- I want to be the most important thing in your life
- If I was good enough you wouldn't want anybody else
- Nobody is going to take my place
- I'll do anything to keep my position

These thoughts can become grudges, and holding on to grudges can result in resentment and lead to a desire for revenge. Envy and jealousy can lead to the desire to destroy the good in another person, through defamation, gossip, and resentment.

At its worst jealousy and envy can be so strong that we find a way of destroying the other person's success.

Prejudice: Sometimes our hearts and minds are closed to people we don't even know. We all have our prejudices. Prejudice is so prevalent in the world that we will take a longer look at this jarring note.

At some point we will form an opinion before the fact, or based on inadequate information. Prejudice is an opinion about something that is different from us: intolerance or dislike toward a group, a political figure, or a particular religion or race. Prejudice is ignorance and fear of a group of people or an individual that is not based on anything objective or concrete. We need to be aware of what we read and hear, because this information can prejudice us against people we don't even know.

Once a stereotype is created, we quickly form an expectation of how someone will behave. For example, a stereotype of a black man might be that he is a mugger, so when we see one we might analyze his behavior in this blurred way. If he asks us for directions or the time we might just ignore him, because we think he is threatening, when in fact his only motive is to ascertain some information.

Prejudice as fear can lead to putdowns, resentment, and antagonistic behavior toward individuals or groups. Where there is prejudice there is an open door for hatred to enter our hearts.

> When we are prejudiced, we violate three standards: reason, justice, and tolerance.... We violate all three standards when we have a scapegoat, i.e. a powerless and innocent person we blame for something he or she did.[23]

When we judge somebody without facts, we are being irrational, acting from our insecurity and fear. We need to realize that to discriminate against somebody because of their race, religion, physical ability, gender, or sexual orientation is prejudice and comes down to our own fears. When we reject somebody for these reasons, we are acting intolerantly, and compassion will be far from our hearts. Sometimes we don't even know the reason for our prejudice. We can meet somebody and take an instant dislike to them based on the way they speak, look, or dress.

Become aware of your thoughts the next time you pass somebody on the street or meet somebody new. Pay attention to them and see how often these thoughts are based on nothing more than your own prejudice.

Prejudice has caused much suffering in the world at large, to the extent that some races of people have been exterminated as a result of delusions about their inferiority. Millions of Africans were slaughtered during the attempted colonization of Africa; millions of Jews were murdered during the Second World War. Millions of indigenous peoples throughout the world have lost their land, language, and sanity due to the rape, assimilation, introduction of alcohol, and genocide committed against them. Jealousy, envy, prejudice, ignorance, and fear of the other have been the driving emotions of such catastrophic behaviors.

Of course we are not directly responsible for these hateful atrocities, but we are responsible for the attitudes and beliefs we now hold. During the twentieth century there was much prejudice in Europe toward Africans, Caribbeans, First Nations, Aboriginal peoples, Indians, and East Asians; in the twenty-first century we can see rising prejudice in Europe toward asylum seekers from places like Bosnia, Kosovo, Albania, and Syria. Islamophobia and homophobia are on the increase in certain parts of the world.

During my early twenties I lived in Billericay in Essex. On bank holidays, those of us who were black dared not leave our homes because we knew the British National Party or the National Front would be out on a rampage. We were terrified and felt the effect of their hatred.

Even today there are places in England where I can be assaulted with racist abuse, and not treated as an equal citizen of the country in which I was born. Racial deaths are on the increase among the Asian and black communities. Black Lives Matter has been a direct response to the police taking the lives of young black men and women in the USA, Canada, and the UK. The slogan "Black lives matter when all lives matter. And when all lives matter, black lives will matter" is a reminder that hatred toward different groups of people is still prevalent in Western society. Similarly there are places where two men, or two women, would not dare hold hands in public because of fears for their physical well-being, or even their lives. Some of the most brutal murders are committed by people who have a prejudice and fear toward transgender people. Prejudice closes down our minds, and hardens our hearts. Prejudice leads to war, murder, and bullying.

You might read this and think you have no prejudices, but sometimes we are not even aware of our prejudiced attitudes or where they come from. There is prejudice in the language we use, and in our thoughts. I grew up being anti-German. Why? Because one of my main carers was a Polish Jew who hated the Germans. I never thought of this as prejudice until I became an adult. Some of us grow up hating the blacks, the Jews, white South Africans (the list is endless), without even questioning it.

Sometimes we have an experience with one person, and then we paint the whole race or group they belong to as horrible. At age thirteen I was one of the few black people on an anti-Nazi march and a policeman singled me out. He asked for the banner that I was holding. I asked him why he didn't go and pick on someone else. I was arrested, taken to a police station, and put in a cell. A policewoman came in, strip-searched me, and asked if I had any weapons. The next thing I knew she was shoving her hand up my genitals. From that moment on I hated the police. I told myself that all police are the same. And I found situations to prove it. My prejudice was fixed. It took another twelve years to begin to look at my prejudice, and thankfully I did, because I only carried hatred in my heart toward the police.

Prejudice is difficult to work with because it is so much part of our culture. All we can do is slowly become aware of our prejudices, be honest with ourselves, and begin to let them go.

 Practice: Reflecting on Prejudice
- Take a moment to think about some people you don't know personally (perhaps those in the media), whom you don't like

or who irritate you. Choose the person you have the strongest aversion to, and list all the things you don't like about them. Then ask yourself why you don't like this person. How have you come to form these opinions? It doesn't matter if you don't have an answer, just reflect on the question for a couple of minutes.

- Look at the list again and ask yourself whether there is anyone else in your life with the same qualities. Ask yourself whether you recognize any of these qualities within yourself. Reflect on this for a minute or two, then look at the list again and see whether there is something you can appreciate about that person. If you're unable to find one good thing, ask yourself why. Acknowledge that this is a prejudice you hold—even if you think you are justified in holding it.

- End this practice by breathing in and out several times, letting go any toxic thoughts that might have arisen.

All these different notes of hatred—from dislike to resentment to envy—will have an effect in our hearts. We need to recognize that they are all forms of hatred, and they all have the potential to poison the love in our hearts. When any one of these notes comes into play, the melody of peace is lost, and the staccato of anger begins thumping around in our hearts. When we can accept that it begins with our toxic thoughts, we are starting to get to know our hatred, and it is only by recognizing our hatred that we can let go of it.

The Taboo

We have seen that it is often taboo to admit to feelings of hatred. We see hatred as the terrain of those who break the normal bounds of our society: pedophiles, murderers, terrorists . . . The twofold effect of this is that as a society we cast the shadow of hatred on these transgressors and don't look into our own hearts to tear out its roots. We need to be able to face this in ourselves, however weak or strong it is, and see our own capacity for hatred and violence. Unless we take responsibility for this part of ourselves, we remain susceptible to it taking us unawares.

This attitude also "justifies" hatred of certain people. We think it is OK to loathe them: "They deserve it." We think we are entitled to hate them. But this is just another more socially acceptable form of hatred, and brings its own consequences. Willard Gaylin, author of *Hatred: The Psychological Descent into Violence*, says, "Hatred . . . may infect others, but it inevitably destroys the hater, diminishing his humanity and perverting the purpose and promise of life itself. No one is entitled to hatred."[24]

As you have just read I once carried hatred toward the police. Twenty-eight years ago I was traveling in a car and passed an accident. My lover at the time said, "Oh no, it's a policeman." "Who cares?" I snapped. "I do," she said. "That could have been my father."

Every harsh experience seemed pointless to hold on to. This was a life, and the person in the accident was an individual. My partner's father worked for the police force. In that moment I could see how I was spreading hatred in the world and I was no different from the skinheads I used to hide from as a child. It took a few more years for me to recognize my prejudice, because sometimes we think we are justified. This is especially the case when we hear about a terrorist attack.

At War

It is above all when a country is at war that hatred becomes acceptable. Politicians, the media, even the general public are not ashamed of voicing their hateful views. In war, hatred is no longer a taboo. We live it, we accept it, and we cultivate it. Hatred is the commodity of war.

During the Falklands War, it was surprising to see how hatred for the Argentinian people became quite acceptable and respectable in the UK, where patriotism was rife and jokes against the enemy were prevalent. Headlines in the British media like "Gotcha" and "Stick It Up Your Junta" became part of the culture. British nationalism became the expression of disguised hatred.

Similarly, during the invasion of Iraq by American and British forces in 2003, I was surprised to receive emails that expressed hatred for the American president, George Bush, and the British prime minister, Tony Blair, from people who identified themselves as Buddhists, Christians, and other spiritual practitioners, as though war gave them the right to hate and as though hateful thoughts, words, and actions were justified and acceptable in time of war.

I, too, was responsible for spreading hatred during the war with Iraq. When I read in a newspaper that an American or British soldier had been killed, I caught myself saying, "Good. Now the Americans and British know what it's like to suffer." I was shocked to hear these thoughts; the ugliness of war had split my heart.

I was angry about the invasion of Iraq. I wanted revenge, and now I was retaliating violently by thinking hateful thoughts. As I heard these poisonous thoughts, I paused and reconnected with the compassion in my heart, remembering that this was a life lost, the life of somebody who had a family who would be suffering just as much as an Iraqi family would be suffering when a child of theirs had been killed.

The reality is that all of us are capable of hatred, though we are not all as likely to feel it or express it in its most extreme form. We may hate for what we believe are valid reasons, but this is still hatred. The danger is that this emotion becomes acceptable, and we tell ourselves we are justified in venting our hatred out there in the world. War is a good example of this. In a world climate of fear and hatred we need to have more awareness of what we are assimilating into our hearts, otherwise our kind and compassionate intentions will become toxic.

Today, when I read on the internet that there has been another suicide bombing, another random shooting in a school or a shopping mall, the first question I ask is, "What happened to this person who was motivated to commit such an atrocity?" I know that if I had been brought up in my country of origin, Sierra Leone, I could have been a child soldier or an adult soldier. I too could have been committing such hateful acts. Nobody is born hating; we are brought up in conditions that contaminate the mind/heart, distorting them. Some of those conditions include growing up in an environment of war, living in a country where you are being bombed or brainwashed, or living among a group of people against whom discrimination is rife. Some of our politicians spout hatred, which sets people at war with one another in their own countries.

Seeing the Roots of Hatred

Hatred is both subtle and lethal. It is unsettling to reflect on how often we are unaware of the hatred we absorb. We can grow up watching people being discriminated against because of their color, sexuality, physical ability, or race and think nothing is amiss, because hateful attitudes are formed in our hearts without our realizing it. There sometimes appears to be so much hatred in the world it is as though it might conquer our capacity to love. But it doesn't; the human heart has a unique ability to love if we can free it up.

Families and Hatred

> If a child lives with criticism
> He learns to condemn.
> If a child lives with hostility
> He learns to fight.
> If a child lives with ridicule
> He learns to be shy.
> If a child lives with shame
> He learns to feel guilty.

—Dorothy Law Nolte

We are born with the capacity to love and to hate. We learn about both from a very young age. Many parents, fearful of the expressions of hatred from children ("I hate you" screamed at a sibling or parent for example), can believe such expressions are seriously wrong or unnatural. If the emotions are gently—or forcibly—quashed by their parents, how then do the children grow up to relate to their hatred? Whatever we keep out has control over us; the enemy we deny has the most power. If, however, we accept that children do experience hatred, we can find appropriate ways to contain it, and our children are likely to grow up to be less violent and much calmer as a result.

By the time we become adults, the word "hate" is not in frequent use in our vocabulary. Hatred is something we would rather forget about, or write off as part of an angry phase in our childhood. Perhaps this is because we have become more aware of the weight behind the word. Instead of freely stating out loud, like a child, "I hate so and so," we keep the thoughts to ourselves. Once we become adults many of us are either too embarrassed or too scared to admit that we harbor hatred. We disassociate ourselves from it, and convince ourselves that hatred lives only in the hearts of criminals.

Learning Hatred

Hatred is not innate, it is learned. We are not born with hatred in our hearts, but we are born into a culture of hatred. We can see the evidence around us. It's in our newspapers, on television, in our communities. Some of us enjoy watching war being acted out on television. Violence has become entertainment. When I explore conflict with young children, some of them say that if it's tough at home they'll take it out on somebody at school. For many of them, fighting in the playground is entertainment; one child said it's like going to a movie. With the advent of mobile phones with video cameras, children will boast about video-ing fights and charge their friends to watch.

The following are some of the ways in which children learn to hate.

By imitation: We know children learn by imitating adults, and if they grow up with violence around them they learn how to confuse hatred and anger with love. When their parents or carers fight with each other, the children witness violent behavior. Some children see their mother being physically abused in one breath, and in the next hear their father tell their mother he loves her. The mother might also tell the child that daddy hit her because he loves her, in order to make things all right for the child. Similarly, if we were hit as a child and told by the adult it's because they love us, we begin to think love is violent, so it is OK to be violent. People who remain in violent relationships have often learned as children that violence is part and parcel of all types of intimate relationships. Another way a child learns hatred is when he or she is physically, sexually, or mentally abused; then the nauseating feelings of powerlessness, vulnerability, and invasion can be so difficult to contain that the strong emotion of hatred can help temporarily quash the fear and pain. Such children begin to internalize their hatred and end up hating themselves.

In fairy tales: Some theories state that children are more able to cope with their lives if they hear the gruesome tales of the Brothers Grimm or Hans Christian Andersen. Some writers, like Bruno Bettelheim, claim that fairy tales are important for a child's development. He believes they help children become powerful in relation to adults, especially in stories in which a little boy has overcome a giant. Although this may be true, I would also argue that fairy tales are often about humiliation or annihilation. The classic children's fairy tales are often based on good and evil. The good person can never do wrong; their behavior is justified, even if it is hateful. It is almost as though they have a right to behave in a way that annihilates another being. While I believe some fairy tales can have a positive effect on a child's development, I'm not convinced that we are completely aware of the effect of some of the more violent and humiliating stories. Are they the best stories to tell children just before they are tucked up in bed? What effect do they have? I know for myself that when I fall asleep after hearing violent or disturbing news, it affects my thoughts, and even how I feel when I wake the next morning.

Video games: There has been much debate whether video games have an impact on our youth. I facilitate an exercise called disagree or agree with some of the youth I work with. I make a statement like: "Video games make young people violent." The youth are always split approximately fifty-fifty. Some argue that video games are just fantasy and it doesn't make them violent. Others state that they have witnessed a brother, sister, or friend become slowly more violent after playing some video games. We may want to ask ourselves: "Why is it predominantly young people under the age of twenty-five who are going into schools and shopping malls and participating in random shootings?" The twenty-year-old who entered Sandy Hook Elementary School in the United States in 2012 and killed and injured twenty-six people had spent much of his teenage years viewing and playing violent video games. They seem to be a risk factor and to heighten aggression.

On the streets: Some people are born into communities where hatred and violence are prevalent. In the film *City of God* (2002), we see how children as young as five and six pick up guns and kill people in the ghettoes of Brazil. In some war zones, the soldiers are little more than children fighting as guerrillas. I have worked in London with boys as young as eight and nine who carry knives and sell drugs, and where it is not uncommon to have a parent or sibling shot dead or killed in a fight. The sexual exploitation of young girls and women and the killing of people and animals are all forms of hatred that happen on the streets.

In the air: Then there is the hatred we just take for granted. Throughout modern British history, police have been called pigs. This language will have an effect on how we interact with the police. Stories passed down from African families about slavery, and from Jewish families about genocide, have meant some people have grown up with hatred toward the colonizer or toward the Germans. In fact, we grow up with so much of how our families may have been wronged, or had to struggle in past generations, it is inevitable that our hearts will be affected.

Personal narratives of hatred: Hatred is all around us and we need to be aware of it. It's in our music, on our screens, in the media. Here are some true accounts of people who came to recognize their hatred.

"I was born into a family of hatred," a friend explained to me. "Hatred was the norm in my family. My mum used the word 'hate' a lot, so we always used the word. There was always a hateful attitude in our home. Everyone in the world was out to get us. Things happened to punish us. My mother did everything with hate. As a young adult I ended up hating the world."

A Buddhist friend of mine said, "I didn't think I had any hatred until somebody suggested I sit down on some cushions and repeat the phrase 'I hate you' as an experiment. I was horrified to see who arose in my heart. I realized there were people I hated, but I had conveniently pushed them out of my mind."

An interviewee told me, "Aged eleven I was aware of hatred. I hated the bus driver who took me to school. One moment he was a friend, and the next moment he was touching me up and saying, 'I don't need your money, that's payment enough.' A few days later at school a friend whose dad worked on the buses said, 'Hey, my dad said you let one of the bus drivers touch you up.' I was mortified. I already told myself I was horrible and dirty, and now this. I hated that bus driver so much that I was pleased when I heard he had died."

Another interviewee said, "I never ever thought I had experienced hatred until I remembered an incident at school. I remember a girl picking on me, and I just exploded and kicked the shit out of her. Although I felt good about it, I remember I was disturbed knowing that she didn't deserve what I gave her. I realize now that I had so much hatred for my dad that when she picked on me I took it all out on her."

When I worked as a journalist I had the opportunity to interview Sinn Féin prisoners in a Belfast prison. I'll always remember one of them saying to me, "What choice do I have? I was born a Catholic in Northern Ireland. I knew I would be killing by the time I was eighteen or I'd be killed. My grandad, my brother, my dad, and some of his brothers have all been killed by Protestants."

 Practice: Reflecting on the Past

- Take a moment to pause.
- Become aware of how you might have been affected while growing up.
- Recall some of the stories that affected your heart.
- Try to recognize which of your prejudices come from your parents, teachers, or the media.

By recognizing our conditioning we can begin to let go of hatred in our hearts.

Hating Ourselves

Many of us find it easier to recognize self-hatred than other forms of hatred. Perhaps this is because we can tell ourselves it only affects us. It's our body; we can do whatever we want with it, and what we do to ourselves is of no concern to anybody else. We often fail to realize that if we hate ourselves it will affect all the relationships in our lives. Everything we criticize ourselves for, we will criticize others for. We will look at our lives, and the world we live in, through the eyes of self-hatred.

All of us probably turn inward some of our natural aggression or frustration during our childhood, and this can later take the form of self-criticism or doubt. Some of us get to the stage of blaming ourselves for everything that has happened to us. Failing exams, not getting a job, the death of a close relative, or parents splitting up are a few of the things we beat ourselves up about. All our weaknesses and mistakes will be included in this self-deprecating list.

We can learn to quell self-hatred by cultivating four basic needs of the heart: attention, affection, appreciation, and acceptance. When we wait for somebody to notice us, we could be waiting forever, and become angrier and angrier. If we know we have done something well, we have to learn to appreciate ourselves, because it may not get noticed. There is nothing wrong for our desire to be noticed, to be given affection, to be appreciated and accepted. We just have to learn to give it to ourselves, otherwise it will keep us on the vicious cycle of self-hatred. When we learn to cultivate these four basic needs of the heart toward ourselves, we will experience our world so differently. We will begin to see things from a place of self-gratitude rather than a place of self-hatred.

Attention

- Bring your attention to your breath.

- As you breathe, imagine your breath carrying kindness, like a beautiful, warm light, filling your body with kindness and well-being.

- Kind attention: With this sense of breathing kindness, give yourself some attention. Just notice your body—the tension and relaxation in the body.

- Cultivate more loving-kindness in your life by just paying attention to yourself. Notice yourself that bit more.

- Note whether paying attention to yourself is pleasant, unpleasant, neutral, or a mixture of all three.

- Sit with whatever arises, as best you can, without judgment or story. Just be open to leaning into the feeling with kindness.

Affection

- Visualize a photo of yourself that you like. Take a good mental look at yourself without judgment.

- Look at yourself with warm, kind eyes. Give yourself a metaphorical or literal hug. Hold yourself and lean into your arms.

- Imagine yourself as a tiny baby, and imagine that you are holding that tiny baby and looking at it with warmth.

- Imagine the weight of this tiny you in your arms. Notice yourself. Squeeze that tiny baby into your being and give yourself a metaphorical hug.

- Cultivate more compassion in your life by looking at yourself, with all your pain and difficulties, with loving eyes.
- Note whether giving yourself affection is pleasant, unpleasant, neutral, or a mixture of all three. Sit with whatever arises, as best you can, without judgment or story. Just be open to leaning into the feeling with kindness. ✿

✿ Appreciation

- Give yourself some appreciation. Allow yourself to appreciate yourself.
- Let sympathetic joy flow toward yourself: appreciate yourself for being on the path, for sitting here and meditating.
- Cultivate more sympathetic joy in your life by saying to yourself, "Well done!"
- Continue to sit with a sense of appreciation flowing toward yourself.
- Note whether appreciating yourself is pleasant, unpleasant, neutral, or a mixture of all three.
- Sit with whatever arises, as best you can, without judgment or story. Just be open to leaning into the feeling with kindness. ✿

✿ Acceptance

- Give yourself some acceptance.
- Accept yourself right now in this moment. Let go of the past, let go of the future, let go of the judgments and the critical voice.
- If they arise, just say to yourself, "Let it go."
- Cultivate more equanimity in your life by saying to yourself, "I am at peace with who I am right now in this moment. I accept myself."
- Note whether accepting yourself is pleasant, unpleasant, neutral, or a mixture of all three.
- Sit with whatever arises, as best you can, without judgment or story. Just be open to leaning into the feeling with kindness. ✿

Wishing These for Others

- Now sit with the strong wish to be free of misery, the strong wish to be free of mental proliferation—the strong wish to be at peace.

- Now extend that wish to all sentient beings; try to feel it on a visceral level.

- Wish that all sentient beings be free from the roots and causes of suffering—that all sentient beings be at peace.

The Habit

Self-hatred is habitual. If something upsets us we are triggered into a recurring pattern of negative thinking. Familiar thoughts replay themselves over and over in our heads. Our alien—the critical voice living inside our heads that we met in the section on anger—hits us with "punch lines" that give us permission to beat ourselves up some more. Some common punch lines are:

- I'm not good enough
- Nobody loves me
- I'm useless
- There's no point trying
- I hate myself

If we could see that our self-hatred stems from layers and layers of pain, and that our punch lines, in the end, are only thoughts, and if we could learn that we need not identify with those thoughts, it would help all the self-hatred in our hearts to dissolve. If we accept that although a thought has arisen, it will cease, the roots of self-hatred begin to loosen. Our alien becomes redundant and no longer has the words to beat us up with. Thoughts are only thoughts, and a negative thought can be changed into a positive one. Letting go of our aliens, our critical voices, our putdowns, will help detox our thoughts and cultivate more self-love within our hearts.

 *Practice: Transforming Our Punch Lines*

- What are your punch lines? You may have caught some of them when looking at "catching your thoughts" in the anger section. See if you can change all the previously listed punch lines, and your own, into positive thoughts. The next time you hear that critical voice, catch what it is you're telling yourself. Ask yourself, "What am I moving away from? Where is the discomfort in my body?" And then breathe. The critical voice can happen so quickly that it may take a few goes; we often beat ourselves up without hearing what it is we criticize ourselves about. We know the way it works: the words keep repeating themselves in our heads, so we think we have no choice.

- Try blowing your punch line—and this negativity—into the universe, where it can dissolve. Now place one hand on your heart and the other on your belly, and say something positive like, "I matter" or even "I love myself." Repeat this at least seven times, then breathe deeply into the pit of your belly.

- Remember that your self-hatred will not disappear instantly; it has taken years to build up and won't dissolve all at once. There is no wonder pill that can change your life overnight. But what can happen is that your self-hatred begins to evaporate as more love for yourself enters your heart.

- To start with, you will begin to hear the whole thought process more clearly. This means you are more empowered to choose whether or not you hold on to the toxic thoughts.

I asked Atula, my Buddhist psychotherapist friend, what was the essence of self-hatred. He said, "Self-hatred is the denial of the good in oneself. It is not being able to accept yourself or any of your good qualities. Self-hatred is the rubbishing of oneself—the annihilation of anything positive."

There was a time in my life when I could see only the negative things in my life, and these are what I chose to identify with. I was unable to experience myself as vulnerable, or indeed positive or successful. Whenever any positive thoughts about myself arose, I swiftly found something to trash myself with.

Many of us who have been bullied, abused, or grown up in abusive households internalize the aggression we experience by being aggressive with ourselves. When we are angry with somebody, we can harm ourselves. Self-hatred can manifest through things like insomnia, migraines, depression, minor recurring ailments, compulsive eating, anorexia, bulimia, drugs, and alcohol abuse—and sometimes this self-harm leads to death. Self-hatred is lethal, especially if we don't pay attention to it.

We can spend many years not loving ourselves because we assume that's normal, because the alien's critical voice belongs to somebody who once had power over us, or because we don't think we have the right to love ourselves. The alien gnaws away at the self-love in our hearts. The resulting self-hatred harms us and everybody around. If we don't love ourselves, people around us will treat us badly. Our whole world becomes poisoned by our self-hatred, and we become the prisoner of our toxic thoughts.

 Practice: Nourishing the Self

- Put this book down, and ground yourself as suggested in other exercises, connecting with either the chair, the bed, or the floor. Always remember to connect with the breath. If a feeling of vulnerability arises, just keep breathing and trust in the process. The feeling will pass.

- When you feel connected with yourself and your breath, imagine a playground full of small children playing happily. You are in charge of their safety.

- Come into relationship with this image in your mind and heart, and just breathe, watching the children play. A child trips and cries for help, so you pick up the child and hug it to your heart. Reassure the child, saying things like, "It's OK to cry" and "I love you," and breathe. Then take another look at the child. As you look, you begin to see reflections of yourself. Keep repeating the above phrases to yourself.

- Whatever feelings well up in your heart, just let them be, don't push them away. Befriend your feelings and tell yourself it is

OK to feel this way. If you start to feel overwhelmed by the unpleasantness, pleasantness, or a mixture of both, open your eyes, allow light into your heart, and say, "I am happy to be alive." If this feels too strong, just say your name.

- This practice might trigger sadness or happiness or feelings that you can't actually give a name to. Just sit with whatever you are feeling, breathing deeply in and out. After each out-breath, try to let go a bit more and trust that even if tears arise they will come to an end, and a new feeling will arise.

- Take a break. Perhaps take a warm bath or call a friend. Just try to be aware if you think you need to reach for food, alcohol, cigarettes, or anything else that might stuff the feelings back down. Give yourself the choice. Part of the process is allowing yourself to feel. Each time it will feel different and hopefully less overwhelming. 🌿

6 🌿 Transforming Hatred

I can't state often enough how important it is, when transforming our hatred, to start by loving ourselves. You might think, "I do love myself," but do you love yourself enough? The more love we have, the less hatred will create a chasm in our hearts. Self-appreciation is the way forward in transforming hatred because to love ourselves we must also learn to like ourselves. When we like ourselves, we recognize all the different aspects that make us who we are. Here is another reflection to help us develop a kinder approach to ourselves.

🌿 Practice: Self-Appreciation

- First of all, connect with your chair by feeling the sensations of your buttocks on it, and your feet connecting with the floor. Or, if you are lying in bed, become aware of your spine connecting with the mattress. Allow the chair or the bed to take all your weight. If you can, recall the first stage of the *metta bhavana* from page 100.

- Imagine yourself on your own, somewhere safe, somewhere beautiful. If you can't do this, just whisper your name. Try to remain aware of your breath and the physical sensations in your body. In your own time say, "May I be happy, may I be well, may I be free from all suffering." Pause for a couple of minutes.

- Now imagine describing your best friend—yourself—to somebody you don't know. Tell them all about your best friend's wonderful qualities. If this is difficult, try to think of one thing you like about yourself and reflect on it. It may be something physical like your hair, or something that you are good at.

- After a while, visualize yourself in a safe, beautiful place and say, "May I be happy, may I be well, may I continue to develop and grow." Pause for a couple of minutes.

- Now become aware of the things you don't like about yourself, one at a time. Every time you think of something you don't like, take a deep breath, and let it go during the out-breath. Choose no more than five things; don't overwhelm yourself. After you have taken an in- and out-breath for each thing you don't like, say to yourself, "May I transform my self-hatred, may I transform my resentment and ill will." Pause for a couple of minutes.

- Try to visualize yourself, or imagine something that reminds you of yourself, then say to yourself, "May I cultivate more self-love within my heart, may I cultivate more kindness within my heart, may I cultivate more happiness within my heart." Once again allow yourself to sit, breathing gently in and out. Then pause for a couple of minutes.

- Try each stage for five minutes. If you don't have time for all the stages, begin with the first, then do one of the others. 🌿

Taking Responsibility

During the sessions on conflict resolution or anger management that I run, we explore the way we use language when we become angry. We look at how taking full ownership of our language is one way to deal with our negative emotions. And we see how hateful and toxic the apportioning of blame and making of judgments can be.

When we are full of prejudice, resentment, ill will, or animosity everything becomes an accusation, and hatred leaks into our hearts.

- You owe me

- You made me do this

- Why do you always do that?

- It's all your fault

What I try to explore instead is how we can express ourselves and be heard, because if we are attacking someone they will either walk away or raise the stakes by accusing us in turn, until all hell is let loose. In the case of young people, this will probably escalate into a fight; as adults we might walk away thinking, "Right, that's it, I've had it with you."

The magic word to move things on is "I." It puts us back into the picture at the same time as encouraging us to take responsibility for our actions. This is a practice used by many people who work in the field of conflict resolution, popularized by the author of *Nonviolent Communication*, Marshall Rosenberg.

Practice: Taking Responsibility

- Think of an incident that has upset you recently, and complete the following sentences. The sentences should be blameless, without judgment, clear, and concise.

- When _____ happens, I feel _____ , because _____ . I need _____ . Would you be open to _____ ?

- When _____ happens: Just state the fact, not your interpretation or the story. Say what happened as an observer might see it. If it becomes a monologue, you have lost the thread. Start explaining it again.

- . . . I feel (I experience) _____ : Name the feeling or experience. Perhaps name the emotions first. Are you angry, frustrated, vulnerable? Or choose a word from the list on page 34. And then ask yourself if this emotion is pleasant, unpleasant, neutral, or a mixture of all three. It may seem strange or unfamiliar to say I feel unpleasant, and you could also say, I experience sadness, or anger, or hurt.

- . . . because _____ : Continue to speak in the first person. Say why it upsets you. This is important.

- I need _____ : Try to identify your needs.

- Would you be open to _____ ?: Be specific. What do you want? This is where you have the opportunity to request something. Ask for something you want to happen or to change. 🌿

Speaking in the first person, in the "I," enables us to keep calm and allows the other person to listen to us. Stating the facts frees us from blame. Not using "you" expressions helps us to avoid accusation. Although speaking like this might not give us exactly what we want the first time round, it will at least open up the possibility of being listened to.

I met up with a close friend to try to sort out the negativity that had been fueling our friendship for years. Resentment, and sometimes jealousy and ill will, often came into play. We went through phases of not talking to each other and being very hostile, which left both of us emotionally bruised. Neither of us wanted to continue like that, but we had fallen into a negative pattern. I had come to my wits' end and decided to stick word for word to what I teach in my sessions and witness the magic. One of our conflicts revolved around the issue of it always being my stuff; it was always my problem, it was all to do with me, which triggered my rage.

When I hear you say, "It's all your stuff, you're the one with the problem," *I experience* upset, because I don't know how to resolve the conflict. I need you to try to listen to me.

Would you be open to hearing things from my point of view without saying it's all my stuff before I've finished?

It was as though she heard me for the first time. She apologized and confessed her part in our communication. I realized that while I could hear blaming speech from my friend, I couldn't hear the blame in my own communication. I had finally become aware of my language and empowered myself by sticking to the word "I."

Speaking in the "I" can help people listen to what you are actually trying to say. It can be the magic word that stops people butting in before you've finished your sentence. In difficult communication, people often find it hard to listen to each other, which escalates the conflict even more.

During a seminar I attended on conflict, one speaker said, "I came from a very angry family. We were always at war. As an adult I sometimes meet up with one of my siblings and within twenty seconds we will be at war. Sometimes I feel on the verge of killing her. Every time we meet we poison each other. Suddenly, one day, I realized that neither of us ever listened to the other; we were always trying to get our point of view across without even hearing the other person speak.

One of us had to back down, so I began to listen and speak in the 'I.' Although it is difficult and unfamiliar, it has started to defuse an old familial pattern of conflict." What is helpful from this example is that the speaker began to see through the story of being always at war. She could see that what was actually happening was that she and her sibling were just not listening to each other. In that moment she could begin to take responsibility for her own actions in the conflict.

Different Points of View

Seeing things from differing points of view is another popular exercise in the field of conflict resolution. I introduce this exercise to the groups I work with. Someone sits surrounded by a circle of people, and I ask them what they see in the middle of the circle. They all see some of the same things, but they also see different things. Sometimes I ask three people to walk around the circle and comment on what they see, and they still describe different pictures of the person in the middle. Most report an interpretation of what they see, rather than the fact that the person is sitting in a chair, wearing a jumper, and so on. Instead they weave a whole story about the person being sad, angry, or lonely.

Life can be very much like that. We can go to a movie with a friend and come away with different interpretations of the story. Who is right? We grow up with siblings and years later, recalling a poignant moment, we disagree. Who is right?

There is no right or wrong when it comes to remembering something. From our point of view it is still a memory. The facts might have become blurred, or our point of view might have become clouded by emotions such as ill will or hatred. Someone recalling an incident when they are angry will tell a different version when they have calmed down. Our emotions influence how we live, think, and speak.

When we can begin to see things from another point of view it means we have let go of our fixed position, let go of some of our anger or hatred, and opened up to the possibility of something new.

When we hold on to fixed views and interpretations of incidents that have upset us, there is the potential for hatred to develop. When we stop struggling with and holding on to toxic thoughts, there will just be a free-flowing energy.

 *Practice: Just Looking*

- Put this book down for a moment and just look straight ahead, becoming aware of everything within sight. When you've noticed what you think is everything, become aware that, in fact, it is just what happens to be in front of you. When we become angry or hateful, our "emotional vision" becomes like this too: we can only see what is in front of us.

- Now look around the room and notice all the things you didn't see looking straight ahead. When our hearts become calmer after conflict, we can look around and start to take in the factors we didn't see in the heat of the moment.

A Case for Ethics

All major religions have tried to protect their disciples from hatred by introducing guidelines on how to live their lives. Christians and Jews have the Ten Commandments, and Buddhists have the five precepts, sometimes called the five mind-training principles.

Ethics are the principles that bring order to a society, group, or culture. Admittedly ethics differ from community to community, but all communities have some code of moral conduct.

When we do something we know we shouldn't, something unskillful, it has an effect on our psyche. Unskillful actions gnaw away at our hearts. They have an effect and we often try to avoid them by blaming others, or by trying to forget them. We can then give ourselves a hard time for not doing the most appropriate thing, or spend time worrying that we will be found out. If we acknowledge that we have been unethical, there is the fear that our happiness might disappear. When we slow down we become more aware of our unskillful actions and can start to develop a relationship with them. We accept that we sometimes mess up, and it's not the worst thing in the world. This thinking can unhook us from the toxic thoughts and help us be kinder toward ourselves.

While working on this book I realized that the five precepts I accepted when I began exploring the Buddhist path, and which I have recited daily for the past eight years, have helped transform my hatred and anger. They have become the training principles by which I try to live my life and have helped to train my mind. The five traditional precepts, with the addition of their positive counterparts, are as follows.

1. I undertake to abstain from taking life;
   with deeds of loving-kindness I purify my body.

2. I undertake to abstain from taking the not-given;
   with open-handed generosity I purify my body.

3. I undertake to abstain from sexual misconduct;
   with stillness, simplicity, and contentment I purify my body.

4. I undertake to abstain from false speech;
   with truthful communication I purify my speech.

5. I undertake to abstain from taking intoxicants that cloud
   the mind;
   with mindfulness clear and radiant I purify my mind.

These training principles have helped me become more aware of my actions. They have helped detox my heart. I am much happier and suffer less conflict. For example, I am more aware of gossiping, more aware of unskillfulness in sexual relationships, more aware of taking things that don't belong to me, and I have chosen not to indulge in alcohol and drugs. All these things contributed to a continuous cycle of conflict in my life.

Of course you don't have to be a Buddhist or take on these training principles. Ethics are a path to a harmonious life. When we are unethical we have a troubled heart and mind; the heart becomes split from the mind.

When we are ethical we have a quiet and peaceful heart and mind; the mind resides happily in the heart. Becoming aware of ethics is becoming aware of our outward actions and of our thoughts and feelings too.

Ethics need no religion; they are part of human culture, and the training principles above are universal and can be applied to anyone.

The Buddhist teacher Thich Nhat Hanh, during his open summer retreats at Plum Village, introduces these training principles as things we could think about moving toward. They are seen as guidelines by which to live our lives. He invites people to take on one of these principles and to go away and try to practice just that one.

Turn back to look again at the training principles. Choose one that resonates with you and try repeating it daily for a week to see if it makes any difference. If it doesn't, you haven't lost anything, and if it does, you have gained something. See them as practical guidelines to help train the heart and mind, to think and feel differently, or as useful tips to help bring more kindness and love into your heart.

A practice of ethics has been one of the things that has helped me overcome the hatred in my own heart. These principles were some of the things that helped me transform my life.

When we try to do something new, like follow the precepts, there is no need to give ourselves a hard time about how well (or not) we are doing. Just by trying, we are beginning to take responsibility for our actions; there is no failing or passing. All that is needed is effort, and we may have to acknowledge that right now we don't have the energy to move toward these guidelines.

With these training principles, there are no rules to break; they are just something we can choose to move closer to in our lives. Remember to take on just one at a time. If we repeat it often enough it will become an organic part of our lives. These training principles can be seen as the basis for all nonviolent communication.

I know that if I could live my life aware of these training principles moment by moment, my world would become a different place, one in which my communication would become the art of the heart. This is a positive thought that I try to reflect upon.

The Power of Mantra

For some people, the thought of sitting down to reflect or meditate, taking on an ethical guideline, or thinking about changing the way they use language can seem quite daunting, even their worst nightmare.

- "My mind is too busy to meditate."
- "If I meditate I might be overwhelmed by sadness or anger."
- "If I start to change my language people will think I'm strange."

These are some of the reasons we give ourselves for not trying the above methods. And they might be valid; different things work for different people. One quite simple thing I've done when I've felt consumed by something negative is chant a mantra. This has allowed me space to take time out from my toxic, obsessive thinking. The power of mantra has helped me detox my heart. Reciting mantras could be seen as similar to repeating an affirmation like "I love myself" or "I matter."

Nobody knows exactly how mantras work, but people who recite them know they have the capacity to purify the heart. It is believed that the sound, resonating through the body, is the very thing that refines our hearts. Mantras are believed to protect the mind from anger, hatred, and fear, and bring about psychic integration.

Mantras are made up of syllables that correspond to the seven main energy points or chakras. Reciting mantras helps bring the seven chakras alive. The chakras are situated between the anus and the perineum, at the sacrum, solar plexus, heart, throat, the point midway between the eyebrows, and the crown of the head.

For centuries, many spiritual traditions in Africa and Asia have used mantras to heal the soul. One of the oldest mantras is the sacred syllable OM. In Hinduism it signifies God and the creation of oneness. It is often used to close a yoga session, and precedes many other mantras. OM is often used to open up all seven chakras in the body. When we chant this syllable it is said that its vibration assists our psychic integration.

Buddhism is renowned for its use of mantra. It is the core practice of the Nichiren strand of Buddhism from Japan. The Nichiren schools believe that if they chant NAM MYOHO RENGE KYO it will bring about great changes in their lives. They believe the three poisons of greed, anger, and delusion will be transformed into compassion, courage, and wisdom. However, there are all sorts of mantras in Buddhism that can evoke compassion, kindness, joy, and equanimity. One of the most famous is OM MANI PADME HUM—the mantra for developing compassion in our hearts.

Practice: A Mantra Practice

- Put this book down and sit facing a blank wall or a lighted candle. Begin to ground yourself, connecting with your breath, and with the soles of your feet and your sitting bones. And just breathe. Put your hands together in a prayer position and raise them to your heart. When you feel settled, try chanting one of the three mantras below for about five minutes. Pause before going on to the next.

1. OM (take a deep in-breath and on the out-breath release the OM, letting the syllable fade with the out-breath)

2. NAM MYOHO RENGE KYO

3. OM MANI PADME HUM

Or perhaps do some research into mantras and find one that resonates with your heart. Then repeat it over and over, not worrying too much about pronunciation, but with the desire to transform your anger, hatred, and fear or the desire for true happiness. If you get tongue-tied, just pause and start again, finding your own rhythm and sound. Chant for at least five minutes and see how it feels. If this feels more comfortable than some of the other exercises I have introduced, stick with this until you feel able to try the others.

A professional peer working in the field of conflict resolution told me the following story. "Chanting NAM MYOHO RENGE KYO saved my life. It alleviated my suffering. I was a very angry child. I was an Asian kid adopted by a poor white working-class family in Shropshire. I was racially abused so much that I often cried myself to sleep wishing I was white. I was badly beaten by eleven white youths during my adolescence. After this my anger took strong hold. I became politically active and caused trouble everywhere I went.

"Wherever I went I was at the center of chaos and conflict. I couldn't fight physically, but I could beat people up with my tongue. My anger dominated everything I did, and I was full of hatred. I managed to find a job where I could remain angry, fighting for community rights. I was so full of hatred that I ended up suing the manager of one of the organizations I worked for, and eventually sued my trade union for not representing me properly.

"I fought with my father, who was a bigot and unhappy most of the time. Then I met someone working in a similar field for racial equality. I was stunned at how compassionate he was, and that he managed to be heard without fighting. Later I discovered that he chanted NAM MYOHO RENGE KYO. He introduced me to the mantra, and since then the inner changes in my heart have been profound. I've undergone a human revolution. This mantra has affected my whole life."

The practice of mantra is strong, and is a path toward transforming the heart. When your head is full of noisy thoughts the chanting of mantras can bring calm to the storm. They have a way of cutting through toxic thoughts and removing their potency.

Loving Your Enemies

> *Hatred is the true enemy; it is the inner enemy.*
>
> —the Dalai Lama

As we saw when exploring anger, we create our worlds in our hearts and minds and we make other people our enemies. We choose not to see someone we don't like when we pass them on the street, we make prejudicial judgments based on gossip and distorted facts, we decide when to like somebody and when not to. Our minds are our own worst enemy.

Our thoughts are what cause us pain. For example, if somebody we love walks out on us, we can choose to begin the process of letting go, wishing him or her well, then rebuilding a new life and finding happiness again. Or we can tell ourselves that this person hasn't really left, that he or she is coming back—then when our desire is not satisfied, we feel pain, anger, and hatred.

After a friend's boyfriend of seven years walked out on her, she was so angry and full of ill will that she wanted revenge. She would sit alone at night and, though she knew she needed to cry, she pushed it down with food and heavy drinking. She was too scared of her pain to just sit with it; it felt too overwhelming.

When food and drink didn't work, she suppressed her tears by hoping he would have an accident. Sometimes she tried to visualize it, which made her feel better.

A couple of months later she learned he had crashed his car. She was mortified, but he survived and made a full recovery. She, too, began to recover. The incident jolted her out of her anger and made her face her pain. Shocked by the accident, she had to accept her suffering, and realized she didn't have to keep on suffering, or cause another human being to suffer. She realized she had a choice: to let go of her hateful thoughts or hold on to them. She could take responsibility for her life and start to loosen her resentment and hatred toward her ex-boyfriend. When she realized this, her heart became much lighter, and after a few months much of her anger had dissolved.

> Everything takes place in our own heart . . . It is enough to know that everything is down to us, and that experiences and feelings, other people, and external circumstances, have no function other than to act as triggers.[25]

"I don't have any enemies, just as I don't have any hatred" is a common notion. On a training course exploring anger and conflict, I was surprised to find myself saying a similar thing when we came to explore "enemy thinking." I had convinced myself that twelve years of regular meditation had eradicated my enemies.

Reflecting on this, I laughed aloud and exclaimed, "I realize I make my friends my enemies." I suddenly realized that, while there weren't any horrible ogres out there, when I think I've been let down by my friends, or when they have not lived up to my expectations, they become the worst people on earth, and I can't bear to think about them. They become enemies of the mind.

Others say, "I don't have any enemies apart from the president or prime minister of my country." This is hatred. If the thoughts and thinking didn't have the president or the prime minister to latch onto, that hatred would find another enemy to latch onto. Hatred is a toxic energy that only has life when it clings and attaches itself to something. It can be acted out on ourselves or others.

Even when somebody makes us their enemy, we still have a choice between seeing them as an enemy or as a friend. The latter will help us be compassionate toward them, and kindness will still flow. If we see that our enemies are our teachers we will see there is still much work to do, and room for more kindness in our hearts.

In chapter 4 I introduced the meditation of cultivating loving-kindness, the *metta bhavana*. The fourth stage of this meditation is called the "enemy" or "conflict" stage. I've regularly used the fourth stage of this meditation to cultivate loving-kindness and free my heart from anger, hatred, and fear. This meditation has been a great healing potion, helping me purify the toxic thoughts I sometimes carry around. It has been the surgery that has detoxed my heart. The meditation has opened my heart and allowed the love and kindness to flow. If you don't think you're ready to face the enemy stage, return to the practice of developing kindness toward yourself, and continue to develop a harmonious relationship with yourself. This is the most important stage, because we must start to feel compassion, love, and forgiveness toward ourselves before we can feel the same toward others.

This is why it is important to start with ourselves in this kind of meditation, so that we can develop positive feelings in our hearts before giving out positivity to others. Don't be tempted to do the enemy stage without completing the first stage of this meditation. Whenever the enemy stage arises in your mind, disturbing you, it is a sign that you need to give yourself some kindness. It's not possible to think kindly about someone if our thoughts are harsh and out of control. If we can remember that so long as we hold on to hatred, our enemy, the person we harm the most is ourselves, we should be able to remember how vital it is to practice loving-kindness. If you only have time to do one stage, just do the first, as outlined on page 100.

 Practice: Developing Loving-Kindness toward an Enemy— A Metta Practice

- Put this book down and ground yourself in your seat. Make sure the seat is fully supporting you and your feet are placed firmly on the floor. Take a little time to reflect on how you are feeling. Then become aware of your breath. Now try the first stage of the *metta* meditation again.

- Start the first stage of the meditation, bringing yourself to mind. Wish yourself happiness and freedom from suffering. When you have completed this stage of the meditation, move into the conflict stage.

- Call to mind somebody who has upset you or let you down. Choose a person you like, but whom you are in a slight conflict with at the moment. Try to visualize them, or visualize something that symbolizes them. Try not to indulge in thinking about what upset you or what is making you angry. These thoughts will arise naturally, but they will cease if you don't indulge them. After a minute, say to yourself, "May she/he be happy," then breathe and acknowledge how you feel. Then say to yourself, "May she/he be well," and breathe and acknowledge how you feel. Then say to yourself, "May she/he be free from all suffering," and breathe. Continue to recite these affirmations with several breaths between each one.

- After five minutes focus on yourself again, and end with, "May I be happy, may I be well, may I be free from all suffering," and bring the meditation to a close. 🍂

If you can practice this daily it will help transform your heart.

Learning to Forgive

> *Hatred paralyzes life; love releases it. Hatred confuses life; love harmonizes it. Hatred darkens life; love illuminates it.*

—often attributed to Martin Luther King Jr.

I once read, in a book on sexual abuse, "Forgiving is not forgetting, it is remembering and letting go." Forgiving is not easy and calls for forgiveness toward ourselves, because as adults we often look back at childhood incidents and blame ourselves for them, giving ourselves a hard time for not protecting ourselves better.

Forgiveness is a way of transforming our hearts. I will explore forgiveness in some depth because it is crucial to our hearts' well-being, and because it can be so excruciating. It is the antidote to both hatred and anger. Forgiveness is the water that can put out the fires of anger and hatred in our hearts. Forgiveness detoxes our hearts.

Most of us know that both love and compassion transform hatred, but reaching the point of compassion, or loving somebody who has ignited pain within us, is a journey that many people can't be bothered with. "What's the point?" some people ask. "Why rake up the past?" In my twenties I often ended relationships at six weeks. When I read my orphanage records, I was stunned to learn that I had separated from my biological mother at six weeks. Without even knowing, I had unconsciously acted something out that had happened in my past. When I became aware of the past, I was able to move beyond a six-week threshold.

Fear often lies behind the "can't be bothered." Some people have held their lives together for so long that they think if they started to delve into the past they would fall apart, and hatred would become a part of their lives; or they fear making the past more of an issue by focusing on it. If people we hate only become issues when we come into relationship with them, and they're not consciously on our minds otherwise, why bother about them?

Of course, none of us walks around constantly with thoughts of hatred toward somebody, but some of us do walk around with hatred stored somewhere in our hearts. Even if we don't feel it all the time, when we are in a relationship with those people, or if we are forced to think about our upset, we have to deal with our menacing thoughts and emotions.

If we have an ounce of hatred in our hearts it will affect everything we come into contact with, just as when there is a war in one part of the world, it has effects elsewhere. We might think it's OK to think ill will toward someone if we don't act it out—after all, there are plenty of people in our lives whom we love. But hatred and love are diametrically opposed; we can't experience free-flowing love if we have any hatred in our hearts.

To start to forgive, we have to move from the belief that hatred, or indeed anger, has protected us against the people who have caused us harm. We often become trapped—holding on to our rage and hatred because we think that forgiveness means condoning harmful behavior. This is not the case. We do not condone, nor do we forget. What we do is let go of our bitterness. In order to do this we have to at least be willing to consider forgiving, even if we are unable to forgive right now. Just by considering the possibility, we have initiated the forgiveness process. If we remain willing to forgive, our hearts will in due course open up. If we don't, we hold on to all that resentment, anger, and hatred in our hearts. If we have a flicker of hatred in our hearts, it has the capacity to pollute not only our relationships with those with whom we are in conflict, but our relationships with people we love. It is also true that if we can't forgive ourselves, we won't be able to forgive others—we will still be holding on to anger and hatred.

Forgiveness is not, as we might think, just a practice for holy or spiritual people. Forgiveness is for all. To love, to be kind, to be compassionate and rejoice in others, is the essence of every human heart. It is just that this becomes polluted from our unexpressed feelings of vulnerability. We need to detox our hearts by learning to forgive. When we detox our hearts we develop compassion.

It's important to repeat that forgiving does not mean condoning or even forgetting. What it means is recognizing that everything is impermanent and nobody remains in a continuous state of wanting to hurt someone, and recognizing that not forgiving, holding on to the hatred, hurts us as much, if not more, than the person toward whom we bear a grudge. We can forgive people and still be aware that their behavior was harmful, and hope that their actions are not repeated. Nothing in life is unforgivable. Even someone who commits murder can be forgiven if we cultivate enough compassion in our hearts.

A sister of one of the children whom Fred and Rosemary West murdered in Britain during the sixties and seventies writes about her journey of forgiveness: "But now, having had the funeral and heard those ghastly details, tremendous rage erupted. It was a pure rage, intense and very physical—a great heat kept rising up from my belly and exploding inside my skull. It was terribly frightening. I realized I was capable of killing, and that I couldn't ever dismiss people who had acted out of a fury like this. So my path toward forgiving began with murderous rage." Later she wrote, "I had lived with this burning question of how to feel compassion for someone who had 'ruined my life'—and in that moment I knew. I experienced a spacious open heart, where forgiving is spontaneous."[26] Forgiveness is difficult to practice. It means remembering and recognizing who and what has caused us pain. The only reward is forgiveness itself, but it is worth it in the end, because happiness can then start to ebb and flow in harmony with the rhythm of a peaceful heart.

Forgiveness for ourselves might sound strange. Why do I need to forgive myself? But if we are honest with ourselves there are things in our lives for which we require forgiveness—even if they are things we consider to be tiny.

 Practice: Forgiveness

- Put this book down for a few minutes and list all the things you have done to cause another person harm, either intentionally or unintentionally. Have a look down the list, and instead of giving yourself a hard time about it, appreciate the fact that you've had the honesty to come into awareness of some of the things that have caused harm. Then, in your own time, say to yourself several times, "In forgiving myself, I remember what I have done, and now I begin to let go."

- You might want to continue writing, or write a letter apologizing to the person you harmed. But don't send it; this is a reflection practice for you. When you come into contact with that person you will find your heart will be more open, and kindness will arise. If it is a friend, there will come a time when hopefully you are both ready to forgive.

- When you have tried this a few times, you could start to think about forgiving somebody. Begin with people with whom you are in communication. Always start with yourself, then call to mind the person you want to forgive and say, "In forgiving you, I remember what you have done, and now I start to let go."

At first this exercise is best used for ourselves and friends we are in communication with, but when we have developed the meditation on metta there will come a time when we run out of friends we need to forgive. We might then become aware that it is perhaps time to include other people who have injured or hurt us. Before we learn to forgive them, we need to develop self-love, kindness, and compassion to support us when we are thrown back onto strong negative emotions. I didn't begin forgiving these "enemies" until after five years of regular meditation, but all that time I was opening up to the possibility, until one day I was ready to forgive. As long as we are on the path of forgiveness, the forgiveness we need to practice will come about when appropriate. Let forgiveness grow in your heart without forcing it.

My Path to Forgiveness

In the Buddhist tradition our enemies are seen as gifts, just as our struggles are gifts; they help us to change. This is not to say we need to create struggles to help us grow; the natural journey of life will bring its fair share of suffering to everyone.

My suffering has been the source of wisdom. Shortly after I was born I went to live in a foster home. At ten months I went to live with another family, then when I was four I was placed in an orphanage, Dr. Barnardo's. At eleven I was sent to live with my biological mother, who mistreated me. I am lucky to be alive. Eighteen months later I was removed by the police and returned to the orphanage. By the time I was fourteen I was living on the streets. At fifteen I was imprisoned and six months later sentenced to a juvenile detention center for shoplifting. I have had to learn to forgive the person who gave birth to me and then tried to annihilate me, as well as forgive all the social workers who failed to listen to me.

While I was visiting Plum Village one summer, Buddhist teacher Thich Nhat Hanh gave a seminar on forgiveness. I was so full of rage and pain. I wanted to be able to forgive but I didn't know how. Through therapy sessions I had begun to let go of my hatred for my biological mother by acknowledging her existence, and accepting that she was alive and was someone I had actually lived with. But I was still angry about having had to live with her, because my life had been at risk. After eighteen months with her I was never the same; I went completely off the rails. I went from being a top student to spending the last of my school days in prison. During a question session with Thich Nhat Hanh I was compelled to speak. I found the courage to stand up and ask, "How can I forgive the person who tried to annihilate me, torture me, who rejected me at birth, who physically and sexually abused me? How can I forgive the father I have never known?"

He looked me straight in the eye, held my gaze, and said with a gentle smile, "Our parents are in us and we are in them. We cannot avoid this. We must find a way to accept them, and forgive them, no matter how awfully they have treated us." He paused and then continued, "You can thank your parents for the strong voice you have, for the strong presence you have, the strong body you have!"

I couldn't listen anymore because I became flooded with compassion. I knew that what he said made sense. I have a strong survival instinct, a healthy body, and a clear mind. My parents' genetic makeup was part of me. I had tried for years to get rid of everything in my body that resembled my mother, and it hadn't worked. Hearing his words penetrated my heart. I knew I had to accept I was part of her. In accepting this I began to accept myself. In accepting my mother for who she was, the poison of self-hatred began to dissolve, and forgiveness took on a new meaning.

With Thich Nhat Hanh's words I left Plum Village with a different mother in my heart. I could see that she too must have been in pain, and had suffered. I knew that the burden of hatred that I had heaped up in my heart for years would only be lifted if I found a way to make peace with my mother. Once we open up to the possibility of connection to the people we need to forgive, the universe provides us an opportunity.

Ten years ago I returned home to a phone message: "I think you are my sister." She had been adopted and nobody knew. I had to tell my two elder sisters who were in touch with our mother. They insisted upon a family meeting. I went begrudgingly, as I had not spoken to my mother for many years. My three sisters supported me when I read my letter, which ended with "I don't know if I will ever see you again." Even though I moved to Canada after that, and thought I wouldn't have any connection with her again, I somehow found the courage to reach out to her. At first I thought I was doing it for her, but the relief I have experienced since I decided to reach out to her tells me that it was for me. In the end, I had to admit that I had a mother.

I had stepped onto the path of forgiveness and letting go. I began to seek ways to detox my heart. It began when I had the courage to tell a therapist what had happened to me during the eighteen months I spent with my mother, things I had told no one, not even the courts. I had held on to so much that it had poisoned my heart. It is incredibly difficult to be happy if we are unable to let go of the things that have triggered our grief.

In emptying out my heart/mind I was able to see the point when I began hating myself. In the orphanage my name was Gruesome. When I went to live with my biological mother she called me *wowo*, which means "ugly" in Creole. One day my mother pushed me to the ground, stamped on my head, reached down to pull my head up, spat in my face, and rubbed my face in the carpet. I don't know why she did this. I was left asking myself, "Why does she hate me so much?" and that became the story that I held on to—so much so that I began to hate myself. I could not let it go.

One day I explored this scene in therapy, and the next day when I was at work with some young children, I noticed an eleven-year-old who reminded me of myself. Her presence reignited my feeling of self-hatred. By the time I left work I was in the throes of self-hatred; I wanted to annihilate the sight of that girl who reminded me of myself and destroy any feelings of vulnerability. Catching this narrative, I was shocked: I had always feared becoming my mother, and here I found myself in her shoes. I understood her actions.

Fortunately, that day I could see things as they were. Turning toward the discomfort, staying with it, forgiveness for my mother welled up in my heart. I could finally let go of the story that she hated me, and see that much of what I had been subjected to came from her own fear and hatred of herself. If she had really hated me, she would not have accepted me back into her life.

Later in life, when I had the chance to read my Social Services records, I saw that my mother was forced into having me. She was a homeless, jobless black woman in the 1960s, and UK Social Services had promised her an apartment if she would keep me. I know deep down that my mother did her best. She didn't actually raise any of her children, and I believe she knew she was incapable of it. The biggest epiphany I had was to see that I contributed in part to the situation with my mother when I went to live with her with a heart/mind filled with hatred and anger. Of course, it is natural to be angry when subjected to abuse, but the fact remains that I fueled part of the dynamic. In acknowledging this to myself my own heart was freed a little more; I was in touch with more forgiveness for myself and for my mother, and apportioned less blame to either of us.

I cannot say that my journey toward forgiving my mother is over.

But I can say that I genuinely have compassion for her. What must have happened in her life that she was unable to raise any of her daughters? Dysfunction has been passed down through the generations from the days of slavery. This is not a justification, but rather a reminder that we should be aware that nobody is born with rage, and that sometimes when people have been abused, they abuse others in turn. And some of us who have been abused end up abusing ourselves. This is why forgiveness is imperative, because it has the power to bring cross-generational dysfunction to an end.

Forgiveness has helped me transform my rage, and although my journey from self-hatred and anger to forgiveness has been traumatic, I am now living my life more fully. My life was full of highs and lows and I was struggling to survive. Twelve years later my heart is happier and lighter. I have now come to believe for myself that the capacity to love, to be kind, to be compassionate, and to rejoice in others has always been a quality of my heart. But I have realized that we can never stop forgiving. It is an ongoing process. The practice of forgiveness is the path to happiness and inner peace.

I came to see how clearly the evoking of my toxic thoughts caused my unhappiness. While I was blaming someone else, I was not taking responsibility for my own actions. I could clearly see that every time I sensed hatred, anger, or fear in my heart, it was a warning that my compassion and love was fading, that it was time to detox my heart, time to slow down and affirm myself and connect with what I have in common with all other human beings. I developed gratitude to my carers because, my auntie Hazel used to say, "We all bleed red." Now it made sense. None of us wants to suffer and feel pain.

I was beginning to see my life from a different point of view. By contemplating forgiveness, I had begun to see more than my own suffering. I could see my mother's suffering, and the pain of others who had triggered my pain. My anger had become free and could now begin to drain itself from my heart, purifying the love and kindness that had poisoned me for years.

Forgiveness was part of my paying attention to myself. When I first began to look at my past, I would never have seen this as self-forgiveness. I wouldn't have known what I was forgiving myself for. But by embarking on the journey of healing, exploring my feelings and my past, the stream of forgiveness had begun to trickle into my heart.

Once we step onto the path of forgiveness the journey never ends. Once you think you have done all the forgiving you need to do, something will come and bite you in the butt. If somebody had told me thirty years ago that one day I would look back at my past and think, "So what?" I would have said, "How can you understand my pain?" But the Buddha's words are true: we can reach a point where we can honestly say, "This is not me. This is not mine. This is not I." Yes, I still have some residue, there is still some more forgiveness to be had for myself and some more forgiveness to be given to my mother. But my heart is freer, so much freer, and happier than it was before I could forgive at all. I no longer have thoughts of hatred when I think of my mother. I sometimes feel unpleasant. In fact, I am occasionally surprised when I hear myself think, "I love her." She is no longer separate and other; there is a compassionate connection between us.

My heart had become toxic by denying its natural desire to forgive. Forgiveness cleanses our hearts. The heart wants to love as much as it wants to cry.

Connecting with our feelings can help us purify our anger and hatred. A heart free of anger and hatred is an accepting heart. An accepting heart is a forgiving heart. A forgiving heart is a contented heart. A contented heart means the heart and mind are in complete union.

Things to Try

- Love and appreciate yourself.
- Nourish yourself.
- Become aware of the signals in your body.
- Remember the things you like about yourself.
- When negative chatter arises, let go of it and become aware that you are feeling unpleasant.
- Try to speak from the place of "I."

- Try to see things from different points of view.
- Know your prejudices.
- Be aware of ethics.
- Practice the training principles.
- Ask yourself who you have made an enemy in your mind.
- See your enemy as a teacher.
- Ask yourself if there is anything you could apologize for, or any unskillful behavior you could acknowledge for yourself.
- Try chanting mantras.
- Forgive yourself.
- Forgive others.
- Develop kindness and compassion toward those you are in conflict with.

7 Replaying Fear

 A Fable

And the mind spoke, saying, "Tell me about my fear."

The heart said, "Your fear is the source of your anger and hatred. Behind your myriad fears is the fear of feeling. This fear attaches itself to many other fears: the fear of losing your life, your identity, your security, your possessions, and of losing control.

"Your fears are your obsessive thoughts.

"Your fears are your vivid imagination.

"Your fears are the anticipation of what may or may not happen.

"Your fear is your inability to communicate.

"Your fear is your irrational hatred.

"Your fear is a delusion that arises from your toxic thinking.

"Your fears have become the ghosts that haunt your heart.

"Your fearful mind has taken over your heart."

My Story: Recognizing Fear

I have had to work with a lot of fear in my life. As a young child I was aware of being scared of dying, because so many people had left me in my early years and I had confused this with death. It wasn't until I grew up that I became more aware how much my fears were rooted in my childhood.

I used to be petrified of mice. I would be paralyzed if I caught sight of one. I would freeze with fear, hold my breath, and numb my feelings. Once the mouse had disappeared, I would start to tremble and my thoughts would become irrational. Out of the corner of my eye I could

155

see mice darting all over the room. Even after I had calmed down, for several days—no matter where I was—I would be looking for mice. I now realize my fear of mice was more to do with their unexpected appearance and their speed, rather than the creature itself. Their sudden swift movement triggered a host of uncomfortable feelings connected with my childhood. They reminded me of the rapidity and the unexpectedness of being beaten as a child. My mother often lashed out at me unexpectedly. It was so quick that I lived on tenterhooks. As a child I would freeze my body, split from all the feelings, so I could cope with the pain and fear of being beaten.

One of the biggest fears I've had to work with, as a consequence of my early life, is my fear of rejection. I had so many people come and go in my life that by the time I was nine I was saying out loud that it wasn't worth getting close to anybody because they never stay. As protection, when people entered my life and disappeared, I would erase their names from my memory. I still have to work hard to remember people's names if they are no longer in my life. At the time it was the only way I could cope.

My fear of abandonment has been the source of many angry outbursts as a young adult. Whenever a lover left me, I would destroy anything that reminded me of them, as I couldn't bear the memories. The only way I could cope with my feelings was by killing them off in my heart. More generally, I was scared of feeling. Even when I parted from a lover after spending an enjoyable day with them, I would provoke an argument with them. Scared of the overwhelming unpleasant sensations in my body triggered by sadness and separation, I managed to jolt myself into the more manageable thoughts of anger by finding fault with my lover. If that didn't work, I would go home and suppress my feelings by bingeing.

My fear of rejection exemplifies the fear of all the feelings I have denied since childhood. These feelings fueled my anger and hatred and corrupted my heart.

These days my biggest fear is connected with the future, fear of the unknown, which is a universal fear. We cannot fix our future, we do not know what is around the corner, we can only prepare—and even that can be scary. Making a will, buying life insurance, and insuring against ill health are courageous tasks. I've learned that fear is part of my life, but it still surprises me when it arises.

Even though I accept I am going to die one day, I still fear uncertainty about my death. I want to know when it will happen, how it will happen; I want to be able to control it. I fear my partner dying. I don't want my partner to die. Although these are natural and common fears, they are my neurotic attachments to things that are not permanent. Even though I can see that Valerie Mason-John is an illusion, is a bundle of identities created by conditions, I still concretize myself. I still habitually turn away from the unpleasantness of aging, sickness, and death.

I work with this fear by reading obituaries in the newspaper or by giving away some of my prized possessions. My partner works away from home, and when we are together, I hold lightly in my heart that this may be the last time I will see her.

I spend time in nature, and try to appreciate the natural cycle of life.

What Is Fear?

Fear is not bad or wrong in itself. It is part of the survival instinct that protects us in times of danger. In its worst form, fear fuels hatred. Some people harm others through fear; others are incarcerated within their own lives, trapped and controlled by phobias that have developed because of fear. Fear reminds us that ultimately we are not in total control of our lives. It is how we handle that fact that matters.

Fear can also be seen as a basic human instinct. It has been said that fear and love are the two innate emotions; all the others are learned. If we don't love, we fear. Fear is the emotion that can trigger us into angry or hateful states of mind. Fear is also a protector, a warning that we have been emotionally disturbed. It alerts us when our lives are at risk.

We are also responsible for some of our fears. We create fear in our heart/minds by how we choose to live in the world. Fear is the opposite of hatred. If we have harmed somebody, if we have done something hateful to someone, we will fear being caught. Some people spend a lifetime looking over their shoulder, afraid of being caught for something illegal that they did, or something they knew they were not meant to be doing.

Fear is frequently the root of both anger and hatred, and can rapidly be disguised as either. When what I will call toxic fear (as opposed to a healthy fear that protects us from real danger) lives in our hearts, we are full of judgments, prejudice, possessiveness, or arrogance—and it is these emotions that throw us into the fires of anger and hatred. If we ever try to put the fear into somebody else, we are acting from a place of aversion. We may want to teach a child not to do something, but we can do that without instilling fear into them.

Fear is the cry of pain in our hearts, the agony of life. When fear arises, our hearts can be split by so much pain that we don't know how to cope. The feelings can become too much for us. Fearing our feelings, we can become numb, and the feelings of vulnerability become polluted with anger or hatred. Our fear is either put on ice or locked in the pressure cooker of our hearts. Without fear our hearts would always be full of love and kindness.

What lies at the root of our fears? We have fears because we are attached to the familiar, we don't want to change, we don't want to let go of our attachments, points of view, habits, or possessions. At root we are scared of dying. As Thich Nhat Hanh says, "We are afraid of death, we are afraid of separation, and we are afraid of nothingness."[27] But if we live, we will die. Most of us fear our own death. Between birth and death, we fear the aging process, the loss of our youth, health, mobility, and faculties. These fears are compounded by fears about loss of our ego, our voice, our visibility—our very selves, although Sigmund Freud believed that what we feared was life, that we feared our very existence.

Whether it is life or death we fear the most, both are inescapable, so we have to find a way to cope. Fear can block out our true, deeper feelings. In the space between birth and death we often block our feelings with painkillers such as work, alcohol, cigarettes, and other recreational drugs, or we can become depressed or angry.

Some fear is intrinsic to our lives, as we don't know what is around the corner, or how long we have to live. In some countries fears are more to do with natural disasters. In most of the Western world we don't fear hunger or death from a natural disaster; our fears are more manmade: assault, robbery, even murder; dying in a plane crash, terrorist attack, or war. For some people one of these thoughts can lead to a multitude of fearful thoughts, and before they know it they have become a prisoner of their own minds—trapped by the things they fear. For example, agoraphobes become prisoners in their homes and in their minds.

Fear can manifest as a ghost, unseen but always hovering. The fear of not knowing, of the unknown, of not being in total control, can dominate our hearts, and our thoughts can become irrational, angry, or hateful. This is when our fear comes fully into action. Fear in action can corrupt our hearts, our lives, our relationships, and whole communities. Many people are born into a culture of fear, and live in constant fear. Fear of violence, their homes being raided, or losing their lives are everyday realities for some people. As a reaction to the ever-present fear, in attempting to protect themselves, some people resort to a life fueled by hatred.

Experiencing Fear

When fear inhabits our bodies, our feelings can be too strong for the heart to accommodate. It feels as though we might have a heart attack, or our hearts might leap out of our bodies. The physical symptoms of anger and hatred are similar to those of fear: we shake, tremble, pant, gasp for air, or become completely rigid. Fear can also be pleasurable and addictive because the body releases endorphins and adrenaline.

Fear makes us vulnerable, which can make us feel like jelly. Our legs tremble, our hands shake, our minds dart about. Sometimes we feel high for several days, then collapse into a depression. Fear can disempower us. In the grip of fear we feel unable to protect ourselves, even physically, which increases our sense of vulnerability. When this happens blame and anger can surface because we know that at least these emotions will make us feel potent, strong, and in control for a while.

Fear is part of life. No one can get through life without fear. We will all have experienced one or more of the above manifestations of fear, but most of us do not sit with the physical and emotional feelings it triggers. We push these back down and allow the toxins of anger, hatred, and blame to invade our hearts.

We often suppress our fear in the belief that we won't be able to cope with such strong feelings, that we will be so overwhelmed we won't be able to get out of bed in the morning. We are afraid of fear. But this reluctance to fear separates us from our hearts. Our irrational toxic thoughts take over, like my thoughts did when I saw a mouse, so that in the end we might not even recognize our own thoughts.

Strangely, considering how difficult we find fear in real life, we often seek it for entertainment. Horror films, thrillers, and fun fairs demonstrate the ways in which some of us allow ourselves to experience fear. We go on a roller coaster, we scream and get off, feel unpleasant with thoughts of throwing up and our limbs wobbling. Ten minutes later we are laughing on the next ride, wanting to experience the fear again. The emotion of fear can feel unpleasant, pleasant, or a mixture of both in the body.

Fear can be exciting, and we know it is fairly safe to experience it at the movies or a fun fair. We can experience the adrenaline rush while knowing it is unlikely that anything awful will happen. For this reason some people are addicted to sports with a high level of risk and fear, like mountaineering, skiing, and whitewater rafting. Fear can be liberating. When I've sped downhill on my mountain bike, knowing my brakes aren't much use, I have experienced spaciousness and a calm sense of peace after I've reached the bottom.

When we touch our fear, we free up space in our hearts, releasing our anger and hatred and making room for love, kindness, compassion, joy, and peace. When we hold on to fear by telling ourselves irrational stories, or when we try to push it away, we destroy our peace and clarity.

In trying to avoid fear, we create ghosts that will haunt us. We must accept that fear is one of those unpleasant things that we will inevitably have to experience. We must face our fears, and let go of them.

Learning Fear

Fear is a necessary part of our childhood development. Healthy fear keeps us out of trouble. The fear of getting into trouble with authority, of doing something illegal, helps to socialize us. We are often quite fearless as children. We learn caution naturally, through the pain and shock of accidents, or when adults alert us to danger. We need fear—of fire, traffic, strangers—to protect us from harm. This type of fear is more intuitive and prevents us from getting hurt.

But there is also the fear used to control children, to make an adult's version of reality dominate, or even—fortunately rarely—the pleasure of seeing this fear. This type of fear can be used to control adults too.

As children, we also learn fear through discipline, rules, and religious doctrine. Some religions have been used to instill fear in children by impressing the fear of God on them, or the fear of hell. In others it might even be the fear of karma. Some religions instill fear of homosexuality, sex before marriage, and mixing with people from other religions, through their persistent teachings on what they consider good or evil.

In terms of discipline, the first time a child is slapped or screamed at, it will experience fear. If children persistently play by an open fire or run toward a busy road, parents may use a slap of the hand to instill fear in them.

Other children learn fear as a result of being different—or being perceived as different—from others. Young children develop fear after being bullied for being fat, black, disabled, or just being a newcomer.

Fears we experience as a child can be played out in similar settings when we are adults. There are many stories about the child who suddenly develops a fear of spiders, or the wind, or the dark. When this kind of fear develops, apparently out of nowhere, there is always something that has triggered it. The birth of a new sibling is a common time for children to develop fears. They may treat their new sister or brother well, but their anger and frustration is acted out through new fears, monsters created in their heads. If this anger isn't released or talked about, frustrated children run the risk of becoming angry and frustrated adults. The same child who was angry or upset about a new sibling might be angry or unbalanced as an adult when someone new joins their social group or workplace. The new person might be a threat to their position or status. Fear will be stimulated but instantly replaced with another emotion.

The Different Faces of Fear

What Do We Fear?

Are we afraid of people who seem different from us, of rejection, of not having enough money, or of being attacked? If we face our fears, they will have less hold over us. Here is a list of some common fears:

- old age, sickness, and death

- losing a limb

- poverty
- accidents
- debts
- losing our faculties

 Practice: Reflecting on Our Fears

Draw up a list of your fears. Try to be honest and don't censor it, no matter how absurd the fears seem to be. When you think you've listed all your fears, read through them and ask yourself how many of these events have actually happened to you. Ask yourself how many of them are ever likely to happen. In the list above, death is the only one that is guaranteed.

Then pause again. This is time for you. Either allow yourself to be guided through the next heart meditation, or just take time to reflect, taking three deep breaths.

Pay attention to your heart. When you feel connected with it, say to yourself, either in your head or out loud, "Breathing in I see my fears, breathing out I let go of my fears."

On the next in-breath say, "I see my fear," and on the out-breath say, "I let go of my fear."

Gently repeat these statements for five minutes or so. If you get lost, just pause, breathe, and start again.

This reflection can help us begin to face our fears. By acknowledging them we can give ourselves a choice between holding on to them and letting them go. So many of our fears do not give us the protection we think they do; they isolate us, and at worst prevent us from living and loving.

We must befriend our fear, looking behind the initial fears and asking ourselves what it is we are really afraid of. Are we afraid of criticism? Are we blaming anyone? The next time you find fear provoked in you, ask yourself whether it is a reality, or something you've blown out of proportion, or a recurring anxiety. The next time you are angry ask yourself whether you are afraid of something, and what conditions have led you to this state.

Types of Fear

See if your fear is one of the following types.

Alarm: This is sudden fear, and occurs when our lives are in danger, or when we sense we are in danger. For example, we become aware that somebody is following us down a dark alley, and our alarm bells start to ring. This is also our instinctual response to change. Our body will have a rush of energy. Many women who have survived an attack have said that they knew something was wrong, that something wasn't quite right, but that they didn't listen to their body. Listen to your body—it could save your life.

Dread: This is fear of some activity: anticipation of something we have done before, or something that is about to happen. It may be as simple as dreading having to eat something we don't like—a common childhood fear—or dreading family reunions or the dentist. Dread is based on past experience that has left us feeling fearful, or anticipation of the inevitable. Let go of this fear—it will consume your mental states.

Distrust: Lack of trust often comes about through fearing what might happen to us. Fear of the government or police can arise from our distrust because of the way they have behaved in the past. Distrust can also be based on false information or ignorance. Remember that our thoughts are not facts.

Panic: This can be momentary or intensifying, as in panic attacks. This type of fear can take us completely by surprise. We might be walking down the street and we see something fall from a roof, or walking in the park when someone comes hurtling past us. In both instances we can panic and become tense. This is our instinctual response to danger. Stop, pause, and take a breath.

Terror: This is a mixture of alarm, panic, and dread, usually when our lives are threatened. We can have all these feelings at once, dreading what might be about to happen. Some attackers terrorize their victims so that they become impotent and unable to fight back. Watch out for the thinking that unravels once you are free from the threat to your life: "I could have been dead, I could have been raped, I could have been killed." This thinking will terrorize you and keep you a victim of your thoughts.

Anxiety: This is a common type of fear in the West. We are anxious about not having enough money, being unable to pay the bills, our children getting sick. Anxiety is actually the inability to remain in the present. When we are anxious we get caught up in what might or might not happen. Go forth from the prison of your mind.

Worry: This is a form of anxiety tinged with fear. We can worry about all sorts of things. The fuel behind this type of fear is often the anxiety that our expectations will not be met, we might not get what we want or feel we need, or we fear unfavorable results. Let go of all resentments. It's been said that expectations are premeditated resentments.

Suspicion: This is a form of fear based on prejudice and mistrust. Suspicion can also be based on false information that makes us fear for our safety or our possessions. Learn to trust yourself, and you will trust others.

Phobia: This is the extreme fear beyond all reason. Phobias can be focused on anything, from dogs, human beings, public transport, to household dust. Phobias often arise when something has been pushed into the unconscious so we are no longer aware what it is. Visit a therapist—they can help you let go of the past.

Clearly there are many things we can fear, and we can be involved in many situations that evoke fear. This next section looks at some examples in more detail, and shows how quickly fear can be transformed into anger and hatred.

A Robbery

One day I walked into my local news agent to buy some stamps. The owners, a husband and wife, were distressed. The wife was just standing shaking, and her husband was clearing broken glass. All of a sudden the wife began screaming, "I'll kill 'em if I ever get my hands on them." The husband continued to sweep up the glass. Another customer came in, and I asked what had happened.

Some local children had run in, stolen some sweets, and on the way out smashed the door. The wife began to say again, "Where are those bastards? I want to kill them." The husband told her no, but the other customer said, "Yeah, they deserve a good hiding. They should be beaten." The wife was still ranting.

I turned to the husband and said, "I'm glad you stopped your wife from going after them, it's not worth it. They could have hurt you even more, some of them carry guns." The wife paused when she heard that word. I looked at her, and she was trembling with fear. I said, "Why don't you have a cup of tea." She laughed and in her native language told her husband to make her some tea.

Observing the aftermath of the robbery I saw her pass through the fright stage, of not feeling, and then, when the shock of what happened had begun to dissolve, she worked herself up into an angry state. Her fear had been put on ice and transformed into hate. Her anger had come from a place of fear, which was very uncomfortable. Perhaps she was angry at being made to feel shaky, tearful. Ranting was her way of taking control of the feelings that she didn't want to feel in her body. Her ranting and raving allowed her to move away from the ickiness of fear. Anger is often a more comfortable emotion because through volatile communication it can mask our vulnerability.

Fear in the World

Have you ever been walking down a road at night on your own and become convinced that in the distance you can see something or someone coming toward you, but when you finally reach it you sigh with relief because it was just some rubbish or an overhanging branch?

This has happened to me many times. I sometimes think I can hear footsteps behind me, but it's just my heart pounding with fear. If someone comes up to ask me the time, or ask directions, while I'm in this state of anxiety and fear, my reply is often aggressive.

Uncontrollable fear is often based on something that has already happened to us. I used to live in an area where street crime is rife. Every day, somebody is mugged for their mobile phone or handbag. Stories of mugging and robbery and murder fill the first three pages of my local newspaper. Even the young people I work with in schools say, "It's not fair, why can't I walk along the street with my mobile phone without being robbed?"

When I was mugged for money, the easiest thing was giving up the money; the hardest was letting go of my fear. Every time someone walked behind me I panicked; every time I saw a youth on the street an angry narrative arose. My feelings of vulnerability became so strong that I couldn't even cycle in traffic. My thoughts started to become irrational and I developed phobias about buses and lorries.

I thought, "What if they had pulled the trigger on me? What if I had been injured?" These thoughts took over my mind and I could see my attacker in every young man who passed me on the street. My toxic thoughts had consumed my heart. I was unable to be kind to any young man who crossed my path.

The reality was that my life had been threatened but I wasn't physically hurt, just shaken. I gradually became aware that this fear was starting to control my life. It was becoming so strong that I was losing something much more valuable than the money; I was losing myself. I had created a story quite different from the actual event.

I realized I had to face my fear if I was to let it go. After several months I went for a walk in the park where it happened. When I faced my fear I felt potent, able to take control of my irrational toxic thoughts. I realized my thoughts were my unexpressed vulnerability. The young men on the streets became individuals again, and I was able to have compassion for myself and my two attackers.

Fear of Flying

A hypnotherapist told me the following story. She was introduced to a client who had visited a number of therapists for help with his fear of flying, because flying was a major part of his work.

The hypnotherapist guided him through his fear. They discovered it came from an old childhood memory. All he actually feared was the clicking of the seat belt; it wasn't flying that caused him distress. The clicking of the seat belt reminded him of the sound of the key being turned when his parents locked him in a room after he did something wrong. When the key turned again to open the door, he feared being beaten.

Years later this fear was triggered by the sound of the seat belt, and the client, unaware of what was being stimulated, panicked at the thought of flying. It was a great revelation, and he could begin to work with the anger about his childhood. This story shows how we can move

away from the facts by misplacing our fear, creating a story that develops into what seem to be irrational fears.

Illness

"Fear has been my cage," said a friend of mine who has spent most of her life in and out of the hospital. When we spoke about fear, I told her there was a time I didn't think she would survive. She smiled. "Neither did I. I was afraid of dying, but I didn't want to live. When I first started having problems with my health, I took a step backward and I fell into a pit. I felt I had been set upon. I lay there in a fetal position with my hands over my head. I kept trying to get out of the pit but I got knocked back. When I looked up, there was nobody at all kicking me into the pit. It was my own fear of being alive which kept me afraid of doing something about my illness.

"I was afraid of being sick, and part of my fear was about facing life as a sickler [someone with sickle-cell disease], lying in a hospital bed in constant pain, regularly pumped with large doses of morphine. Whenever I had the slightest bit of stress in my life, the hands would go up over my head, and I would end up back in the hospital with a sickle cell crisis. One day I looked up from my hospital bed and saw there were no attackers there. They were all in my head, and I was stuck because I had been holding all the fear in my head."

My friend admitted she was angry about being ill, angry at how sickle cell anemia had taken over her life, angry that nobody believed she was ill, and angry with the way the medical profession treated sickle-cell patients. She realized her fear had held her prisoner. She was a victim of her own anger. The moment she looked up and saw there were no attackers was the moment she came into relationship with her ghosts. She could see that the feelings of being set upon were not feelings at all, just a story she had created to make sense of her painful and tough situation.

She found the courage to crawl out of her pit, and although she still has severe sickle cell crises, they are fewer, and her attitude has allowed her to become happier and more content.

Fear is the hardest of all toxins to dilute. Just like conflict, living with some form of fear is part of life. Our methods of managing our fears often cause their own problems, because we either blow the fears out of proportion or unconsciously move into resentment, judgment, prejudice, and ill will—the components of anger and hatred. Because anger and hatred are often the disguising of our fears, we have to let go of our anger and hatred before we can begin to face our true fears and come into relationship with our vulnerable feelings. If we hold on to our anger and hatred we will be forever haunted by our fears.

Fright, Flight, or Fight

Most of us have a limited repertoire of responses to fear. We traditionally talk about flight or fight. We can take flight, often in a type of autopilot mode, which can very practically help us to survive a life-threatening experience. Or we can be jolted into the fight mode, and fight for our lives like a cornered animal.

In my experience there is a third response, when the body goes into fright mode before we are booted into one of these ways of coping. Some people don't get beyond the fright stage, while others, in seconds, make the transition to the survival instinct of flight or fight.

Fright mode is the place where we connect with shock. When we are in danger we automatically experience fright. In fright mode our bodies feel the panic physically: our hearts miss a beat, our knees buckle from fear, and we freeze, we might even wet ourselves, or worse! The fright mode numbs all our thoughts and feelings. It is one of our first reactions to a trauma.

When we experience fright, we are unable to experience the unpleasantness of the state of fear, so in a matter of seconds we freeze all the feelings that invade us. This numb state can help us cope in the short term, but if we become stuck, rather than move into flight or fight, we remain like a moth caught in a lamp.

When fright begins to loosen its grip, we might move into states of anger or hatred. We can look at the stages of fear like this:

Fright: This is the moment of physical threat or trauma. We are frightened. Our hair might stand on end. We can freeze, faint, and get stuck, eventually connecting with anger or hatred to shift us from this frozen state. This is the beginning of fear. Some of us may have an adrenaline rush and move swiftly into flight or fight. Even if an inanimate object triggers fear, we can still freeze our feelings.

Flight: After the fright, the brain kicks into gear, adrenaline is released, and some of us have the capacity to cope with the situation as though it was our everyday job. In flight mode, our body, mind, and heart have the amazing capability to go into autopilot and coast through an incident completely calm and in control. We are rational, controlled, and the energy released gives us the ability to cope calmly and easily. When the flight comes to an end, we are often left feeling unpleasant after the situation has been dealt with, and we unconsciously or consciously move into anger or hatred to help us shift away from these feelings.

Fight: After fright, if we don't flee, we are jolted into fight mode. This is the animal energy that comes alive in us to help us cope with a trauma or threat. Just as a tiger would fight for the survival of its cubs, we fight to protect ourselves. Our body is capable of doing a lot to keep alive. We can even have the strength of an elephant in fight mode; the primitive survival instinct comes into play. However, we can still move into fear once we have survived the situation. Toxic fear normally sets in after these stages. Fear is toxic thinking: "What if . . . ? Just imagine if . . . If only I hadn't . . . If nobody had found me, I might have . . ." Toxic thinking is like a predator chasing the goodness out of our hearts. When this happens, fear takes a grip, and hatred and anger lurk in our hearts.

The Invasion of Fear

We saw above the ways we cope with a frightening episode and how our fear becomes toxic. But it is when a threatening or traumatic situation has ended that fear really begins to take over our hearts and minds. During the trauma we feel adrenaline run through us, a natural reaction. It is after the trauma that fear can become negative, anxiety sets in, and we can become heads without bodies. At this point, everything takes place in our heads. Fantasies about what could have happened start to take over, especially when we're lying in bed trying to get to sleep, or woken up by the memory of a frightening event.

When we experience fear, we must be aware of this aftermath when we turn over and over what might have happened, replaying the event and stoking our fears. This is when our toxic fear can turn into full-blown hatred. This delayed reaction is the insidious fear that begins to corrupt our hearts. Once the shock begins to fade, the feelings rise back to the surface.

Instead of trying to accept, and sit with, the unpleasant nature of our feelings, we let the rational mind take over, going over all sorts of thoughts about what might have happened. That's when fear invades our hearts, throwing our minds into whirlwinds of anger and hatred or other strong emotions.

"You have to stay with fear. If you push it away you can't get rid of it. The more you push it away, the bigger the fear becomes," said Ratnasuri when I interviewed her for this book. "Fear comes from the inside. When I went on my first-ever solitary retreat, I was terrified. When I stayed with the fear, I realized I wasn't afraid of anything externally, it was all on the inside. The fear was in my head. Once I realized this, I stayed with the fear and it transformed into bliss."

Many of us fantasize about being caught up in a disaster. This state of mind can even occur when things are going well for us. We start to fantasize about all the awful things that could happen. Or we fall in love, and within the space of an hour fantasize about the entire relationship with one or both of us ending up in some tragic accident. Modern city living can also play havoc with our minds; I've heard friends say they live in fear of being murdered, raped, or mugged.

Many of us experience anxiety every time we walk onto the street. Every day we hear or read about an act of violence in the news. I was stunned and sobered by a story I read in my local paper not long ago. A young woman had been robbed of her handbag while standing at a bus stop with her child. She was so furious that she ran after her attacker and retrieved her bag. She returned to the bus stop, and when her bus came she boarded with her child, but her attacker managed to catch up with her, and as she tried to board the bus he repeatedly stabbed her. She survived, but her attacker got away.

I was stunned by this story because many victims, surviving their attack, start to fantasize about what they could have done, or what they might do if they saw their attacker again. This woman, so enraged by her attack, found the nerve to fight back for what was hers, and paid an even bigger price.

The attacker instilled fear in the woman, and she responded with what one might call justified anger. His anger, hatred, and fear were acted out in a rage, probably motivated by his lost sense of identity and his pride, hurt by his victim's unexpected retaliation.

When we become the victim of an attack, it destroys all the defenses we have put up to keep people out. Once the shock has dissolved, we are left with a whole suitcase full of vulnerable feelings. These feelings are so potent that it seems the only way to deal with them is through anger and hatred, or by shutting out all our feelings. What we keep out begins to control us.

Although our fears could become reality, they usually remain the invention of our own minds. We need to be aware that when we create these fears, our thinking can unconsciously lead us to the very thing we fear. Our thoughts have an uncanny habit of creating our worlds, so we must become aware of our fears, and try to let go of them.

Twenty years ago I was swimming in the sea off the Greek islands when I saw what I thought was a shark. I panicked and swam like mad. And then I burst out laughing, because the shark was a floating log, and I had not moved an inch with my frenzied front crawl stroke. Fear can immobilize us.

The following story came to me while I was trying to understand my own relationship with fear. While sitting and reflecting on my fears, I could see this story, which illustrates a spiral of fear, being lived out in many people around me.

The Invaded Hearts

There was once a young woman and young man who fell in love at the age of sweet sixteen, and when they turned twenty-one their parents allowed them to marry. They were so in love that they became the talk of their small town. They were the ideal couple. They did almost everything together, and never got on each other's nerves.

After ten years of marital bliss, things started to change. They still loved each other very much, but boredom began to creep unawares into their hearts. One day the man came home from work and announced, "Guess what I think we should do? I think it's time we had a baby." His wife froze with fear when she heard this idea. She trembled and her palms became sweaty. Her husband had never seen her like this, and comforted her and asked what was the matter.

She soon recovered and when they sat down to their evening meal she said, "Darling, I've been thinking about what you said. We can't have a baby."

"Why ever not?" her husband replied with surprise.

"Because if we have a baby things will change. What's more," she said, "it may die, and then we will be unhappy for the rest of our lives," and she wept.

"I hadn't thought about that. Perhaps you are right," the husband said, and he went up to bed with this thought on his mind.

The next evening when he returned from work, his wife ran up to him, gave him a big hug, and said, "I've been thinking about what you said. Why don't we at least have a dog."

Her husband began to shake and sweat. His wife was quite startled by his reaction and went to hug him again.

"No, we can't have a dog," he blurted. "It will change our lives, or it may die, and we will be unhappy for the rest of our lives," he said, and he wept.

His wife consoled him and agreed with everything he said, and they both went to bed with these thoughts on their minds. In the morning, his wife wouldn't let him get up.

"Not now, darling," he said. "It's time for me to go to work."

His wife replied, "I've slept on our conversation last night, and I've decided I don't want you to go to work anymore."

"Why ever not?" her husband exclaimed.

"Because you might get run over by a car and die, and my life will change, and I will be unhappy for the rest of my life."

"I hadn't thought about that," her husband replied. "Perhaps you are right. I will tell my boss I won't be coming to work anymore. I'll stay at home with you."

They both got up together and had breakfast. While the wife was clearing the table, her husband said, "Let me do that, darling, it's great to be at home and help for a change."

"OK," replied his wife, "I'll see you later."

Her husband looked astonished. "Where are you going?"

"I'm off to the gym, and then to have my hair and nails done, and pick up some shopping."

"You can't do that."

"Why ever not?" she replied.

"You might get attacked and end up dead in the gutter. My life will change, and I'll be unhappy for the rest of my life."

His wife sat down and said, "I hadn't thought of that. Well, we can order all our food over the internet, and I can work out to a Jane Fonda video, and we can pay for somebody to come round to do my hair and nails. I'll stay at home with you."

Then they sat beside each other looking out of their front room window not feeling very happy at all. A whole day passed, then another and another. They stopped eating and drinking. They didn't even move from their seats. They fell asleep in their chairs, and when they woke, still sitting rigidly in their chairs, they were still overcome by fear.

One evening, the wife became restless. She started trembling and pointing at the window. Her husband was puzzled, for there was nothing there. All of a sudden his wife let out such a scream that all the neighbors came running to see what the fuss was about.

The husband took her hand and asked, "What's wrong, my darling?"

"Look," she said, and she pointed. "There are monsters coming toward our house."

"Don't be daft, it's just our neighbors coming to see that everything is all right," her husband said, and he let out a big laugh.

She held on to his hand so tight and said, "I'm scared."

"Scared of what?" he asked.

"I've been thinking, I don't want you to die first, because everything will change, and I will be unhappy for the rest of my life." And with these final words she slumped in his arms and died.

Her husband looked out of the window, and he too could now see the herd of monsters stampeding toward his house. He panicked. He was convinced the monsters had killed his wife. He ran to a cupboard in the kitchen, pulled out a pistol, and from his window shot several people on his front path. He put the pistol to his head, but he collapsed before pulling the trigger; he was too frightened even to die.

He was sent to prison, where he lived the rest of his life in fear, still convinced the monsters had killed his wife, and that they were now trying to kill him. 🍃

The *Book of Tao* says we have as many fears in life as we do in death. This story is a metaphor about the roots of our basic fears: the fear of impermanence and the fear of extinction—change and death. This couple ended up living in fear of living and in fear of dying. They were resistant to change. In the end it was fear that separated them.

This couple's fears represent what many of us manage to keep at bay every day: fear of losing a child, a partner, or comfort, and fear of dying. There is a saying that to ensure happiness we must die before our children and die after our parents. The one thing parents dread is the loss of a child before they die. What this couple feared, they brought into being. Change and unhappiness were brought about by their fears.

Their life was extremely comfortable and they managed to keep their fears at bay until the possibility of a third party was introduced into the relationship, which then began to spiral into chaos. The wife's panic may have been her unspoken fear of change, or of something new spoiling what she already had.

Fear of the Unknown

We fear things because we are attached to the familiar. We don't want to change. When something new or unfamiliar enters our lives we can feel out of control, when in fact we are thinking we are out of control. If we change, we may lose a sense of ourselves. Instead of acknowledging our fears of anxiety, we can become angry and blame everything in sight. This is our ego's protest.

For example, if I am working as a secretary and I am told by my line manager that the communication systems are to be upgraded by computerizing all the diaries and phones, this is a major change and I panic. I am given six months to learn the package. But I like the old system, it works for me, and what if I'm unable to learn the new one? I become angry with my line manager. Why wasn't I consulted? But I don't say anything, I just seethe, and think of ways to sabotage the new system. In the end I have to back down, but instead of facing my fear I hand in my notice and look for another job.

In this way, fear begins to control my life and actions. I risk leaving and finding a new job every time something unfamiliar is introduced without my consent. I could keep on running, but eventually there will be no job to run to. What do I do then? Become depressed, angry, bitter, or seek revenge on all the employers I believe made my life a misery. This might sound extreme, but there are people who feel driven by their fears. It can be a hard place to be, sitting with the unknown, not feeling in control of the future.

Fear of the unknown is a reality. We are not in control of what happens from moment to moment, but we can become present to every moment by connecting with our thoughts, feelings, and physical sensations. This will give us all the control we need to take care of any new or unfamiliar situation in which we find ourselves.

Fear of Difference

Fear of difference generates prejudice, and therefore hatred. As discussed in chapter 5, prejudice covers a broad spectrum, from race to culture, sex, disability, and much more.

Fear of difference is rooted in ignorance. I vividly remember, at the age of ten, visiting a seaside town in Essex with some friends. My best friend had asked if I would go with her to visit an aunt who had once worked at the children's home we shared.

There were four of us, including us two black kids, walking through the seaside town looking for her aunt's house. We were walking down a street and coming toward us were two white kids aged about four and five. They screamed and ran like the wind in the opposite direction. We were so surprised by their reaction that we chased after them.

One of the white kids I was with found them hiding behind a bush. They told him they were scared his black friends might catch them, boil them in a pot, and eat them. He let out a big laugh, and we came running up. The two kids were quivering behind the bush. Our friend said, "Look, they're OK, they don't eat people," but the kids had run away and were nowhere to be seen.

As adults, if we fear difference it will often be acted out aggressively. When a black family moves into a neighborhood, white families might move out. When a disabled person asks to be served in a shop or restaurant they can often be ignored, and when an out homosexual walks along the street, he or she might be attacked.

It is a tragic irony that, though traveling from country to country has become easier over the past thirty years, in some countries the fear of difference has escalated. Some governments in Europe have clamped down on refugees entering their countries through fear of being invaded. The refugee from Albania, Romania, and Serbia has become the new black in England. Even some black people are down on refugees. Fear of difference keeps us in our own little worlds. At its worst, we start to fear anyone who is not a blood relative.

Being with Fear

While out socializing one evening, a friend of a friend told me this story and gave me permission to tell it. Something woke her in the middle of the night. She felt uneasy in her body, and decided to get up and make herself a drink. As she entered her hallway she felt a cold breeze, looked into her front room, and noticed the window was open.

Thinking she must have left it open before going to bed, she went to close it. To her surprise there was a man standing in the middle of the room. She knew in that moment that she had two choices. She could scream and throw something, or she could remain calm, confident, and compassionate.

"If I screamed, I knew it might make him nervous and he would attack me, so I automatically chose the second option," she said. She spoke to him, asked him if he needed any help, and he ended up staying a couple of hours, talking at her kitchen table and eating soup and bread. He left through the front door.

"It seemed natural to be calm, I felt sorry for him, and he responded to my compassion. We were both in danger. My martial arts practice has taught me how to deal with danger."

A day later she received a letter from the man, who thanked her and said that nobody had ever listened to him before, and would she like to meet up. She passed the letter to the police.

"The interesting thing was the reaction from my friends. I had to work hard at not being afraid of being in my own home. My friends said I should sleep at their place, but I knew if I did that I would start living in fear. It helped that I was moving anyway in a few months, but I faced my fear, just like I face the knives that come at me while I'm training in martial arts."

I was struck by this story, and how she knew that she had to face her fear. She made a split-second choice that stopped her from moving toward anger and hatred. Many people would have gone into fight mode: flipped out, thrown the first thing that came to hand, screamed.

If the intruder had retaliated they'd have fought back. Others would have flipped into flight mode and run.

Once the incident was over, despite her friends and their toxic thoughts and anxiety, she didn't move into toxic fear. She didn't replay the story over and over and ask "what if" questions. She faced her fear and let it go. She said, "I knew I was lucky and I appreciated that. I knew it was a one-in-a-million chance that it happened to me. The likelihood of this happening again was slim, and if it did it would just be bad luck."

Her thought pattern unhooked her from her toxic thinking, and she avoided terrorizing her mind with what could have happened. Anger and hatred was far from her heart. She said she felt compassion for this man.

More importantly, after the incident she was able to free her mind from all the thoughts of what might have happened. She didn't stoke her thoughts, or indeed fan them. She was able to cope with her vulnerability while not being abused.

This is a unique story, and I'm not suggesting we all begin making friends with our intruders. Nevertheless, it demonstrates how somebody worked with staying in the present moment, becoming aware of both their own and another person's feelings.

We too might be thinking right now, "She was lucky, look what might have happened." But thinking what might have happened can just trigger us into some kind of story or fantasy, or an angry rage. Instead, try to focus on what did happen and the positive outcome, because in this case nothing awful happened.

Most of us would not have the capacity to be with fear in the same way as this woman. Even if we managed the situation calmly, most of us would then move into the phase of intoxicating ourselves with what could have happened, which might then throw us into a rage.

Coping with Fear

Because of our fast and full lives, many of us have found short-term ways to cope with fear to help us get through the day. Some of us use anger, others anesthetics like smoking, food, drugs, and alcohol. Some of us avoid situations in which our fears might arise, like public transport or eating out.

In the performance world, I have watched many people have a stiff drink or take a line of coke before going in front of their audience. When I first started out as a journalist, I was often asked to do public speaking. In the early days I remember my heart pounding so much that it felt it was breaking out of my body. I would drink a double vodka and everything calmed down. Instead of facing my fears, staying with the uncomfortable feelings, I just stuffed everything down inside. You might ask what was wrong with stopping myself from being nervous. There is nothing wrong with not wanting to be nervous, but there is a cost to me in having to turn to alcohol every time I feel vulnerable in public situations. I risk becoming dependent on alcohol and at worst becoming an alcoholic.

Many of us become angry in a panic, for example, if we are stuck in traffic and are going to be late for work. Some of us swear at the dashboard, blame the driver in front, or pick a fight with whoever we are traveling with. Deadlines make us panic, especially if we are working on a computer and it crashes, or the printer starts acting up. I've watched people try rebooting a computer by thumping it on the screen, or kicking a printer in frustration.

When we cover our fears with these coping mechanisms, we are unable to come into relationship with the vulnerable feelings that need our attention. Coping with our fears means becoming aware of what we are actually afraid of. To manage our fears, a transformation has to take place in our hearts, just as with anger and hatred.

My friend Ruth died at age forty-two. We had known each other since we were twenty-three. We partied and took drugs together, and I watched her raise her son. She was given five years to live, and then after a botched surgery was told, "Sorry, it's actually only a matter of months." I spent a lot of time with Ruth and her ex-partner/coparent of her child. Eventually, amid all our discussions of Ruth's inevitable passing and memorial service, her ex said, "This is ridiculous! Why are we waiting to celebrate her when she's dead? Let's do it now. You ask her: you're the Buddhist."

I sat beside Ruth's sickbed, held her hand, and said, "Your friends would like to celebrate you now, give you a living funeral. What do you think?" Without hesitation she said, "Yes! I want something to help me pass over to the other side." So we planned it together. She was clear about who she wanted to be there, and about what food and drinks to serve. She was clear that people were coming to say goodbye to her, and she was saying goodbye to them. Her mother, brother, and his family all came. Her partner at the time was nervous, and thought Ruth was too sick to go through with it. I sat by her bedside again and asked Ruth if she wanted us to cancel it. She sat up and emphatically said no. She wanted to face her death with her friends.

As I witnessed her mother say goodbye to her daughter, and all her friends, I was infused with courage. It seemed the most normal thing for all of us to be doing on that day: publicly rejoicing in our friend. Ruth died two days later, and left me with the courage to face my own death when it arrives. Ruth's death continues to remind me that there is nothing to fear. Death is just another event in life—one that we cannot avoid—so we may as well face it and embrace it.

Things to Try

- Make a list of all your fears.
- Each time you face a fear, breathe, recognize it as a fear, and let it go.
- Listen to your body.

8 🍃 Transforming Fear

A heart full of fear is a heart full of toxins. Anger and hatred will definitely contaminate our thoughts. Detoxing our hearts from fear is no
different from detoxing our hearts from anger and hatred. After the
event that triggered feelings of fear, when we are safely back home, we
need to pause, take a few deep breaths, watch our thoughts, and listen
to our bodies.

If we are to take care of ourselves when fear arises we need first
to allow ourselves to sit with the uncomfortable physical sensations.
Through reconnecting with our body we also allow ourselves to feel the
physical sensations of our emotions and become aware of our thoughts.
Pema Chödrön comes back again and again to the need to stay with our
experience, no matter how uncomfortable. "When we practice meditation we are strengthening our ability to be steadfast with ourselves.
No matter what comes up—aching bones, boredom, falling asleep, or
the wildest thoughts and emotions—we develop a loyalty to our expe
rience. Although plenty of meditators consider it, we don't run screaming out of the room. Instead we acknowledge that impulse as thinking,
without labeling it right or wrong. This is no small task. Never under-
estimate our inclination to bolt when we hurt."[28]

In Buddhism it is said that connecting with our bodies, physical feelings, emotions, and thoughts is the foundation for happiness. When we
become more aware of our physical sensations it is hard not to be aware
of our bodies, thoughts, and emotions. Each time a physical sensation
arises we will have a response to it, either craving or aversion. If we feel
discomfort in our bodies we are likely to push it away. If we feel comfort
in our bodies we are likely to crave more and cling to it. We react to our

thoughts and feelings in the same way, and when we don't allow ourselves to experience them fully they end up getting stuck in the body.

When I don't allow myself to experience my feelings, they manifest as pain. When I am sad, I feel it physically in my throat, as if I am choked with tears. The pain in my body is the blockage. If I allowed myself to cry, the pain in my throat would cease, and my thoughts and feelings would eventually cease too. Coming into relationship with my body has been a great healer. Not only has it helped me like my body more, it has helped me let go of my fear. Physical exercise, at the gym and in yoga sessions, has helped in this process of putting me in touch with my body and my breath.

Those of us who are not inclined to physical activity can also come more into relationship with our bodies by just sitting and connecting with our bodily sensations. Try the physical sensations practice on page 54 again. When you become aware of fear, ask yourself what stories you are telling yourself right now. Stick to the facts. What are you actually feeling? If you feel physical discomfort, again ask yourself what you are thinking right now. Try not to react by tensing up even more. Keep sitting, and let go of any toxic thinking.

Nothing can be lost through slowing down and connecting with your body, its physical sensations, emotions, and thoughts. Instead, there is a lot to be gained. We can begin to understand how our minds work, alert ourselves to when we are feeling vulnerable, become aware of our negative chatter, feel that we do matter, and in the end have a much happier and contented heart.

Kindness to Strangers

Being different can be the source of fear, prejudice, and full-blown hatred. In working with our prejudices around difference we can use the meditation on loving-kindness of which I have introduced some of the stages in the last two chapters. The third section of this meditation introduces the neutral person, somebody we hardly know, someone we might see regularly but pay little attention to, for example, a bus driver, shopkeeper, or a beggar.

Bearing in mind somebody we hardly know is perhaps the most challenging of the stages. It can be surprisingly scary to think intimately about someone like that. Focusing on a stranger in this way is something we wouldn't normally do. Prejudice might arise as we think about them, even some aversion, so this part of the meditation is quite profound. It has changed my relationship to beggars on the street, for example. I don't live in fear of them anymore; I see them as human beings like me, who are trying to make a pound or two in this crazy world. The third section of this practice challenges our fear of difference from others.

 Practice: Developing Loving-Kindness toward a Stranger— A Metta Practice

- Take a few deep breaths, put this book down, and ground yourself. Make sure your seat is fully supporting you and that your feet are placed firmly on the ground. Then become aware of your breath permeating your whole body.

- Try the first stage of the metta meditation as outlined in chapter 4. Begin the first stage of the meditation by calling yourself to mind, wishing yourself happiness, and feeling kindness toward your suffering. Once you have completed this stage, move on to the following new stage of the meditation.

- Call to mind somebody you hardly know, someone you might pass on the street or at your workplace. Choose someone toward whom you feel very little emotion, positive or negative. Perhaps bring them alive by imagining their fears, frustrations, desires, and dreams. If this is hard just try to visualize them and remember they are human like you and they do not want to suffer. Try not to indulge thoughts of how odd or invasive this feels. These thoughts can arise and cease naturally if you don't indulge them. After a minute, say to yourself, "May she (or he) be happy," then breathe and acknowledge how this feels. Then say to yourself, "May she (or he) be well," then breathe and acknowledge how this feels. Then say to yourself, "May she (or he) be free from all suffering." Then breathe, and continue to say these three phrases with several breaths between each. After five minutes bring this meditation to an end and celebrate the fact that you have faced a fear, the fear of difference.

- Come back to your breath. Gently come back to your surroundings, look around you, and pause. Reflect on what you have just experienced. 🌿

Accepting Change

When we begin to consider our true fears, we see they are all connected with loss or change, which amount to the same thing. If we can accept impermanence in our lives, our hearts will slowly become free from fear. If we can accept that things will change, that we won't always be as fit as we were, that not all our friends and family will be alive by the time we reach our sixties, we might be able to start to free ourselves from the toxic grip of fear. When fear loosens its grip we become free of judgment, criticism, blame, and anger. A fearless heart is a heart filled with compassion.

In my early thirties I worked very hard to let go of my bulimia nervosa. My head was full of thoughts like, "If I let go of my bulimia who will I be?" It had been part of my identity for half of my life. I was too frightened to let go and change, and I continued to beat myself up with the binge-purge cycle. I had convinced myself I could only function when my life was in chaos. If the bulimia went, there would be no more drama in my life. Who would I be? Holding on to this fear, I held on to my bulimia. My bulimia was my anger at the world and my self-hatred. I wasn't ready to change; I didn't want to change. My anger and self-hatred was the fear pumping through my heart. It was the toxic energy that kept my hatred and anger alive. Can't change, won't change? The reality is we are always changing.

Our lives are as unpredictable as the British weather. When it rains I try to be positive, to see the good things about the downpour and wrap up well so I can enjoy it. When changes occur in our lives we could do the same: try to find the positive in the situation, and wrap up well, as we are vulnerable when changes come about. Wrapping up could mean slowing down, allowing ourselves extra sleep, allowing time to experience our feelings.

Several years ago I was struck by the beauty of dying flowers, which most people throw out. I decided the next time I bought flowers I would observe the process. I was so overwhelmed by compassion as I watched some of them age, some quicker than others, that I realized these flowers were teaching me the universal law of impermanence. The venerable Sangharakshita writes, "Our bodies are like flowers; one day they will wither and die."

 ### Practice: The Practice of Flowers

- Get some flowers and put them in a vase. Put them in your bedroom so you can see them daily. Do whatever you want to keep them alive. Become aware of their beauty while aware of their slow death. Pay attention to them every day—their color, shape, scent—and watch how they change, age, wither, and die. Watch how some of them remain bright while others fade. Even after you have decided they're dead, leave them in a vase for a couple more weeks, or as long as you can bear, and watch how they deteriorate further.

- See these flowers as a metaphor for you and your friends. Think about friends around the same age as you. Become aware whether some of them have gray hair while others do not, whether they look older or younger than you, or fitter, and that some of your friends may already have died.

- Reconnect with your breath, look at the flowers again, and reflect on their life process. They age much faster than us, but if you can engage with these flowers every day, and be aware of them moment by moment, they can teach you the inevitability and beauty of life, decay, and death. Through this practice we can start to discover that we have a choice between facing our fears with love and compassion, or with blame, anger, and hatred. I do this every time I buy flowers.

If we could maintain the awareness, and the tension, of knowing that things are in constant flux, we would live our lives differently. What would it be like to live every day as though it were your last? To face the fear of the unknown while realizing that every day could be beautiful? The Native American Indians have a saying, "Today is a good day to die." This is a strong practice, as many of us have regrets. Perhaps it's an even stronger practice to say that every day is a good day to live, because in doing so we must come into relationship with change.

Opening Up

One day we will all have to face our worst fear, the fear of dying. It is inevitable. Do we just dread it, or do we avoid any thought of it? Or is there a way in which we can prepare for this ultimate change? The regular practice of watching flowers is a step in this direction. Some parents buy their children pets so that they can come into relationship with death.

Every separation, every loss, is the beginning of something new. Stephen Levine, the author of *Who Dies?*, says that "every separation is a mini-rehearsal for our own death." Every separation has a tinge of sadness or relief. Coming to the end of a book, a movie, a holiday, a meal, even a day's work, can leave us with unconscious thoughts of sadness, which can feel unpleasant in the heart/mind and body. And some separations can be really traumatic, such as losing a loved one, the end of a relationship, a child leaving home. Can we learn from any or all of these? One of our lessons is that we really do not know how long we have in this life.

Six years ago several people I knew died of various illnesses. Then my twenty-eight-year-old assistant dropped dead. I was so shocked by the suddenness, without any warning, that his death had a long-lasting effect on my life. I realized I didn't really know how long anybody would be around. I started telling people in my life that I loved them and valued them, and even set about trying to resolve long-term conflicts. I also started doing all the things I wished I'd done, visited the places I'd always wanted to visit, wrote that novel I'd been wanting to write for years. Initially I panicked. I thought, "Help! Am I going to die?" But many years later I am proud I had the courage to do those things, because I realize fear had been one of the factors stopping me. I also thank my personal assistant for teaching me this lesson. Sometimes I can say it is a good day to die, as well as a good day to live, and one day maybe I'll be able to say every day is a good day to die or to live.

We shall not cease from exploration
And the end of all our exploring

Will be to arrive where we started
And know the place for the first time.[29]

If we could see what T. S. Eliot saw—that things are cyclical—or become aware that there are no endings, only separations and new beginnings, these perspectives might give us more space to actually live our lives, and live them in full color. I believe that even death is not an end, it is a separation from this world and a movement toward something new and unknown. Admittedly we don't know what that will be, but when we are born we have no idea what our lives will be.

If we opened up our hearts to our feelings it would free our hearts from fear. We must be prepared to feel our feelings and let go of them. Then we must face our fears, one by one, gently and slowly.

Among the many stories about the Buddha is one in which he sent his disciples into a forest to meditate. After trying to meditate, his disciples came running back, very frightened. When the Buddha asked what all the fuss was about, the monks said they were too scared of the awful animals and monsters lurking in the forest.

The Buddha sent them back into the forest, but before he did so he gave them a tool to work with their fears. The tool he chose was the metta bhavana, the meditation on loving-kindness, the development of positive states that we have been practicing in this book. The fact that the Buddha chose this practice speaks highly of its power to soothe fears. And in this story, the disciples did go back and meditated for hours.[30] When you have compassion in your heart, there is no room for fear.

If you have read all the other chapters, it is time for you to try the whole meditation of cultivating loving-kindness for yourself, a friend, a neutral person, an enemy, and for all beings. If we are able to develop more love and kindness in our hearts, the toxins of anger, hatred, and fear will evaporate, and our hearts will be filled with compassion for all humanity.

 Practice: The Complete Practice of Cultivating Loving-Kindness—The Metta Bhavana

- Pause, ground yourself, and connect with your breath, your sitting bones, and the soles of your feet.

- Call yourself to mind, and with kindness say, "May I be happy. May I be well. May I be free from all suffering," pausing between each phrase. Repeat this several times over the next five minutes.

- Then call to mind a friend, saying gently, "May they be happy. May they be well. May they be free from all suffering." Remember to pause between each phrase, repeating the phrases several times for the next five minutes.

- Then call to mind a neutral person and say, "May they be happy. May they be well. May they be free from all suffering," and after five minutes let go of the neutral person.

- Bring to mind an enemy of the mind, somebody who typically causes you to lose peace of mind when you think of them, and repeat the process, saying, "May they be happy. May they be well. May they be free from all suffering."

- Once all four stages have been completed, call to mind yourself, your friend, the neutral person, and the enemy. Visualize them, and be aware of all four. Perhaps extend your hand to the friend and the friend receives it. Then the friend extends their other hand to the neutral person and the neutral person receives it. The neutral person extends their other hand to the enemy of the mind and this person receives it. The enemy of the mind extends their hand to you and you receive it. All four of you are connected and interconnected. Then say, "May we all be happy. May we all be well. May we all be free from all suffering," pausing between each phrase.

- After about three minutes, focus back on yourself and start to spread the loving-kindness out to all your family, saying, "May all my family be well. May all my family be happy. May all my family be free from suffering." Then focus on your friend and let the feeling expand out to all your friends, saying, "May all my friends be well. May all my friends be happy. May all my friends be free from suffering." Then focus on the neutral person and expand your feelings to include all the people you don't know, saying, "May all the people I don't know be happy. May they all be well. May they all be free from suffering." Then focus on your enemy of the mind, expanding the loving-kindness in your heart to all your enemies of the mind, saying, "May all my enemies be well. May all my enemies be happy. May all my enemies be free from suffering." Finally, wish all beings happiness by saying, "May all beings be well. May all beings be happy. May all beings be free from all suffering."

- Then become aware of loving-kindness detoxing your heart by visualizing light beaming into your heart. And accept that your heart opened up as much as it could, and the discomfort of thoughts will cease with time. 🌿

Things to Try

- Know your fears.
- Be aware of your toxic thoughts.
- Try not to replay incidents over and over again.
- Connect with your body and all its physical sensations.
- Sit with your feelings.
- Welcome the stranger.
- Accept change.
- Regularly get flowers and observe them dying.
- Open up to loss and aging.
- Find a positive in every change.
- Begin to live some of your dreams.
- Practice cultivating love and kindness for yourself, friends, strangers, enemies, and all sentient beings.

9 The Cultivation of Happiness

A Fable

And the thoughts spoke all at once, saying, "Tell us about happiness."

The heart said, "Happiness is my true nature. There is no other way I prefer. Happiness is a heart free of anger, free of hatred, and free of fear. A heart full of love, kindness, joy, and peace is a contented heart. These are the heart's natural response to myself and to all humankind. When anger or fear arises, I don't cling to it or stoke these emotions, I let go of them, otherwise my heart may ignite in full-blown hatred. When I have achieved this, my heart and mind can start to merge as one. A happy heart is a feeling heart. A happy heart is a calm mind. A happy heart is a heart free from toxic thoughts. A happy heart is aware of choice. A happy heart can accept change. A happy heart craves nothing. A happy heart clings to nothing A happy heart is an accepting heart. Your happiness will come and go.

"Where there is happiness there is sadness too. Accept that your happiness will ebb and flow, and one day you will wake up with a heart full of happiness. When sadness arises you'll be able to be kinder toward it. Then it will not stay as long, and new feelings will arise. This is the universal law of letting go. You will find your happiness in the present moment. There is nothing more for me to say."

My Story: Recognizing Happiness

One night, at the age of thirty-six, I lay awake with fear. "I can't go on living," I said to myself, "I can't make it." I had just arrived home from a hedonistic week in Rome. I had slipped and the bulimia had flared up.

As I lay awake that night I really believed I wasn't going to make it. Then a small voice from nowhere said, "Yes you can." Instantly, my alien spoke louder: "I can't, I'm a failure." The small voice that for so long I had been unable to trust spoke to me again. "If you want to, you can. You have a choice." I gave myself a hug, and let go of the self-hatred that had been beating me up for seventeen years. I didn't need the bulimia anymore. My anger, hatred, and fear had begun to dissolve.

This was the turning point in my psyche. If I wanted to live, I could. If I wanted to let go of the bulimia, I could. It was me who had been holding on to it. It had served its purpose, and I didn't need this coping mechanism anymore. But freeing ourselves from our addictions is one of the most frightening and liberating things we can do.

I chose to let go of my second from last major intoxicant, bulimia. I had let go of alcohol and drugs a few years earlier, but I couldn't see that I had only lapsed into fear. I couldn't appreciate that the accumulative practice of meditation, and working in therapy for the past eight years, had had an effect. I was no longer the same person. I had learned to pause and respond to the issues that arose to test me. Instead of relapsing and spiraling down into a dark hole full of negativity, I lapsed. I acknowledge my slip, picked myself up the next day, and consoled myself, instead of letting my toxic thoughts give me a hard time.

But this lapse had taught me there could be no time off in the healing process; it is a lifetime commitment. When we begin to nurture love and compassion in our hearts, we start to see the real work we need to do. We bring choice back into our lives, and the drama of our lives begins to slow down. We begin to see that perhaps the biggest intoxicant of them all is our own thoughts.

When I realized that my biggest intoxicant was my thoughts, it gave me a new lease of life. I could see how I had identified with my thoughts so much that I became my toxic thoughts. I didn't want to be my thoughts anymore. Although they could still intoxicate me, I realized I could abandon my thoughts, create new ones, and embrace true freedom of heart. This new way of thinking is a challenge. As in other areas of our lives, we need to take responsibility for the way we think.

We create our lives in our heads, and spend our time trying to live those lives. We become angry and resentful when they don't go to plan.

A Gift

If I could give something to all human beings it would be the reminder of the breath and the gift of meditation. When we become aware of our breath we slow down. The breath is all we need to meditate—whether it is a long breath, a short breath, or a raspy breath. When we meditate we become more aware of ourselves and more aware of the things we need to do. Meditation is a heart, mind, and body detox.

Meditation spring-cleans our hearts. It dusts off the cobwebs that have collected over the years. When we first begin to meditate we may be fortunate and dwell in blissful states, or it may feel overwhelming because all the things we have suppressed in order to function come to the surface. This may mean we will come face-to-face with our suffering. Rather than seeing this as self-pity, this can be the beginning of compassion for ourselves.

Meditation can help us cultivate more long-lasting compassion, love and kindness, joy, happiness, and peace within our hearts. If we could just stop for a moment and take three deep breaths, we would allow ourselves to connect more fully with our hearts, feelings, and then our thoughts. This can be enough to start the process, and when we have more time we can consider just sitting and meditating for a short while.

Detox Hints

Every individual will have their own approach to the attainment of happiness. Pause for a moment, and in your own time make a list of all the things you do to make yourself happy. Try not to censor or criticize yourself, just try to be honest and appreciate the fact that you have liked yourself enough to try and bring more happiness into your life. After you have made the list, choose the most constructive and healthiest, and perhaps introduce more of these things into your life. If you were unable to list healthy ways of cultivating more happiness, try not to give yourself a hard time, just acknowledge this and see if you can find something you can do from the following list.

The Buddha used a raft as a metaphor for his teaching, and said, "Take the raft as far as it will carry you, then abandon it."[31] So when something doesn't work, or stops working, just try something different.

In other words, if what you're doing right now hasn't been working, find the courage to try something different. Some or all the things listed below may help soothe the heart. They are practical suggestions intended for those of us who have a busy life. They are kind reminders of some of the things we have explored in this book, as well as a few other suggestions. If this is the section you've chosen to flick through first, try some of the ideas and see where your heart takes you.

 Practice: Time Out

- Take three deep breaths when you wake up, in the middle of the day, and before you fall asleep.
- Remember to pause, even if it means stopping whatever you are doing for five minutes, or pausing between finishing one task and starting the next.
- At the end of the day try breathing in happiness, joy, and peace on the in-breath, and breathing out all the toxins you have accumulated during the day on the out-breath.
- Do one of the reflections or practices in this book at least once a week.
- Take up meditation.
- Go on a meditation or art retreat.
- Visit your local Buddhist center, church, mosque, temple, synagogue, or a park bench, and just sit and reflect.

Get Fit

- If you use public transport to get to work, try walking or cycling part of the way once a week.
- Go for a brisk walk or a jog once a week.
- Visit your local gym.
- Go to a yoga or Pilates class.
- Go for a swim once a month.
- Go to a five rhythms class once a month.

Enjoy Home

- Take a long shower or bath.
- Create a special place in your home where you can sit or lie quietly.
- Go to bed early once a week.
- Listen to music that helps you feel peaceful.

Take Care of Yourself

- Drink plenty of water.
- Eat regularly.
- Watch your caffeine, sugar, nicotine, alcohol, and drug intake.
- Cut down on your consumption.
- Exercise once a week, either swimming, yoga, or at a gym.

Appreciate Yourself

- Learn to love and affirm yourself more.
- Connect with physical sensations in your body.
- Explore therapy.
- Book a massage, shiatsu, or reflexology session.
- Visit your local sauna, spa, or steam room.
- Visit a flotation center.

Appreciate Beauty

- Visit a local water feature and sit there for a while.
- If you live near a river or large pond, take a walk there at least once a fortnight.
- Visit the countryside or the seaside or sit in your local park.
- Visit your local art galleries.

Embrace Change

- Try not to use "You always . . . ."

- Try to speak in the "I."
- Explore the possibility of changing yourself.
- Experiment with letting go of some past hurts.
- Explore the willingness to forgive.

Always Breathe
- Remember to breathe, allowing yourself to experience the breath fully. If you only have time for this, intermittently taking a deep breath throughout your day will slow you down and have a positive effect on your heart.

We are coming to the end of this book, and there will be feelings and thoughts. Whenever we come to an end of something there can be a mixture of the four feelings I have written about in the book. When we avoid these feelings, emotions of elation and/or anxiety can arise. And we can make judgments and interpretations, experiencing this book with dissatisfaction, abandonment, and other emotions. Take this opportunity to tune in to what it is you are actually feeling. Perhaps take one more moment to reflect. Remember to breathe.

Ask yourself whether your living conditions are supporting you in being happy, and whether you are taking care of your anger, fears, and hatred. For example,

- Are you happy with your life right now?
- Are you happy where you live?
- Are you happy in your job?
- Are you happy in your relationships?
- Are you happy if you're single?
- Are you happy in yourself?

If the answer is no to any of these questions, it might mean that something quite major in your life will have to change. If you say it can't change now, be aware that you have made a choice to hold on for whatever reason. If you have answered yes to all these questions, just ask yourself what made you pick up this book and read it. Maybe the change has already begun to take place.

If you are now thinking, "Gosh, I need help," look for it. There is nothing wrong in therapy for the body, heart, or mind. Paying someone to massage you or to talk to can be a nourishing experience. The therapist is a feature of Western lifestyle. Our families might have become disparate and our friends so busy that there is nobody around to talk to. Be creative. If you think you can't afford it, put it out to the universe. Opening up to change can bring about positive surprises.

Negative mental states can be an addiction. I call it "addiction to stinking thinking." Some people laugh and say that's not an addiction. Gabor Maté, author of *In the Realm of the Hungry Ghost: Close Encounters with Addiction,* says that addiction is "any behavior, substance-related or not, that brings temporary pleasure or relief; a behavior one craves but is unable to stop despite negative consequences."

Physical and emotional pain takes place in the same part of the brain. Our stories, interpretations, and judgments are often an attempt to make sense of a situation and to soothe or escape the pain. Our stinking thinking can be temporarily pleasurable and have negative outcomes too. It can be a matter of life and death. It can be the cause of road rage, domestic violence, sexual and physical abuse, bullying, self-harm, prejudice, murder, and war, and may even sometimes lead someone to take their own life.

Remember the Sky

It might seem that some of us do have more sunshine in our lives than others. Yes, shit does happen, and some of us have it easier than others. In the end we all suffer, and our pain is immeasurable, and if we try to compare our lives with others, we will suffer even more.

If, when we are suffering, we can literally look up to the sky, we will eventually discover some sunshine again. If the clouds are gray, they will change. So too the painful thoughts that have polluted us will, one by one, slowly disappear. The sky is free and there is enough for everyone.

Happiness and sadness are part of the same deal. Accept your sadness and be patient; it will pass. Try not to grasp at happiness; there is nothing there to grasp. This just means being in the present moment, with your body, your mind, your heart, observing your feelings and thoughts, arising and ceasing, just as though we were looking at the clouds. Happiness lives in all of us. It is like the sun. It shines in you and in all other sentient beings.

We are always changing. We are just holding on to photographs of our lives.

The Buddha reminds us that everything is impermanent, and that reality is perfumed with compassion. Tears fell from my eyes when I first read these words. They gave me hope, and awareness of the toxins I had to start to let go of. When I started to remember my hurts, I realized I could let go and even contemplate forgiveness and moving on, and detox some of my moldy toxins.

When our hearts detox, our thoughts are purified and our minds are replenished. Our hearts then have the capacity to start cultivating love and compassion toward ourselves and others.

Try letting go of your toxic thoughts the next time you feel hurt. Trust in your heart. Trust in the process of impermanence. Trust in the practice of self-love. Detox your heart.

NOTES

1. Gary Snyder, *The Real Work: Interviews and Talks 1964–1979* (New York: New Directions, 1980), 17–18.
2. Ryokan, *One Robe, One Bowl*, trans. John Stevens (Boston: Weatherhill, 1977), 23.
3. Ray Scraggs, *How to Be Happy* (New York: Brixton Books, 2002), 50.
4. Patrick Whiteside, *The Little Book of Happiness: Your Guide to a Better Life* (New York: Rider, 1998), 34.
5. Marshall B. Rosenberg, *Nonviolent Communication* (Encinitas, CA: Puddle Dancer Press, 1999), 15.
6. This list is adapted from one developed initially by Theresa Holman for the Clean Break Women and Anger Programme. Clean Break is a national theater company that works with women in prison; women in the mental health system; and women at risk of using drugs or alcohol or being physically, sexually, or emotionally abused.
7. Galway Kinnell, "Saint Francis and the Sow" in *Three Books* (Boston: Houghton Mifflin, 2002).
8. Adapted from a list developed by Theresa Holman for the Clean Break Women and Anger Programme.
9. James Hollis, *The Eden Project* (Toronto: Inner City Books, 1998), p. 22.
10. Adapted from a list developed by Theresa Holman for the Clean Break Women and Anger Programme.
11. Adapted from a list developed by Theresa Holman for the Clean Break Women and Anger Programme.
12. Thich Nhat Hanh, *Anger: Buddhist Wisdom for Cooling the Flames* (New York: Rider, 2001), 117.
13. Suzy Austin, "Have you got 'hurry sickness'?" http://www.dailymail.co.uk/health/article-186676/Have-got-hurry-sickness.html.
14. This model is a handout included in *Playing with Fire—Training for the Creative Use of Conflict*, by Nic Fine and Fiona Macbeth, a manual containing a

sixty-hour course designed for trainers of staff working in youth clubs, residential homes, special needs centers, the penal service, volunteer projects, further and higher education, and any other environment where conflict can become an issue.

15. Pema Chödrön, "The Answer to Anger and Aggression Is Patience," *Shambhala Sun* 13, no. 4 (March 2005): 33.

16. Juan Mascaro, trans., *Dhammapada* 1–2 (London: Penguin, 1973), 35.

17. Thich Nhat Hanh, *Anger*, 3.

18. From Ayya Khema, *Dharma Life* no. 19, http://www.dharmalife.com/issue19/crossthedivide.html.

19. Pema Chödrön, "The Answer to Anger and Aggression Is Patience," *Shambhala Sun* 13, no. 4 (March 2005): 35.

20. From Ayya Khema, *Dharma Life* no. 19.

21. *Dhammapada* 222, p. 68.

22. Willard Gaylin, *Hatred: The Psychological Descent into Violence* (New York: Public Affairs, 1993), 234.

23. Honglin Zhu, "From Intercultural Awareness to Intercultural Empathy," http://www.ccsenet.org/journal/index.php/elt/article/viewFile/9671/6919.

24. Gaylin, *Hatred*, 234.

25. Ayya Khema, *Come and See for Yourself: The Buddhist Path to Happiness* (Cambridge, UK: Windhorse Publications, 2002), 117.

26. *Dharma Life* no. 22 (2004): 21–22.

27. Thich Nhat Hanh, *No Death, No Fear: Comforting Wisdom for Life* (New York: Rider, 2002), 19.

28. Pema Chödrön, *The Places That Scare You: A Guide to Fearlessness in Difficult Times* (Boston: Shambhala Publications, 2002), 38.

29. T. S. Eliot, "Little Gidding," in *Four Quartets* (New York: Harcourt, 1943).

30. Commentary on the *Metta Sutta*, Paramatthajotika 9.6–9.

31. *Alagaddupama Sutta*, Majjhima-Nikaya 22.13.

FURTHER READING

Dalai Lama. *Healing Anger*. Ithaca, NY: Snow Lion Publications, 1997.

Hay, Louise. *You Can Heal Your Life*. New Delhi: Full Circle Publishing, 2003.

Holder, Jackee. *Soul Purpose: Self Affirming Rituals, Meditations and Creative Exercises to Revive Your Spirit*. London: Piatkus Books, 1999.

Mason John, Valerie, and Paramabandhu Groves. *Eight Step Recovery: Using the Buddha's Teachings to Overcome Addiction*. Cambridge, UK: Windhorse Publications, 2013.

Paramananda. *Change Your Mind: A Practical Guide to Buddhist Meditation*. Birmingham, UK: Windhorse Publications, 1996.

Rosenberg, Marshall B. *Nonviolent Communication: A Language of Life*. 2nd edition. Encinitas, CA: Puddledancer Press, 2003.

Salzberg, Sharon. *Lovingkindness: The Revolutionary Art of Happiness*. Boston: Shambhala Publications, 2002.

Sangharakshita. *Living With Kindness: The Buddha's Teaching on Metta*. Birmingham, UK: Windhorse Publications, 2004.

Thich Nhat Hanh. *Anger: Buddhist Wisdom for Cooling the Flames*. New York: Rider, 2001.

Titmuss, Christopher. *Transforming Our Terror: A Spiritual Approach to Making Sense of Senseless Tragedy*. London: Godsfield Press, 2003.

ABOUT THE AUTHOR

Valerie Mason-John, MA, was born in Cambridge in 1962. She was awarded an honorary doctorate of letters for achievements in her lifetime and for her contribution to the African and Asian diaspora. As a journalist she covered a range of stories—from Aboriginal land rights and deaths in custody to prisoners in Maghaberry Prison, Northern Ireland—and she was a weekly feature writer for several newspapers in the UK. She has written two books documenting the lives of African and Asian women in Britain, written and produced several plays, and published a collection of prose and poetry. Her debut novel, *Borrowed Body*, was published in 2005 and won the Mind Book of the Year Award. Her book, *Eight Step Recovery: Using the Buddha's Teachings to Overcome Addiction*, won the category of the best self-motivation book in the 2014 USA Best Book Awards and the 2016 International Book Awards. *The Great Black North: Contemporary African Canadian Poetry* won the best educational book and best poetry book in the 2014 Alberta Book Awards. She is the cofounder of Healing and Insight, an online teaching faculty that explores the sharp edges of suffering through the lens of the Buddhist teachings. She also codesigned the Mindfulness Based Addiction Recovery six-week course, along with the trainer. She coproduced Blackhalifax.com, fifteen short stories about the history of the black pioneers of Halifax, Canada. She was the winner of the Windrush Achievement Award as Arts and Community Pioneer 2000 and of the inaugural Shorelines Competition for Black British African, Asian, and Caribbean writers. She currently works as a trainer for anger management, anti-bullying, restorative justice, mindfulness, and conflict transformation.

The author is a devotee of meditation and yoga and is a member of the Triratna Buddhist Order, formerly known as the Western Buddhist Order. Based on the west coast of Canada, she travels internationally, leading retreats and delivering training. She is available to teach workshops and give talks on the themes outlined in this book. She can be reached at detoxyourheart@gmail.com.

12 Steps on Buddha's Path
Bill, Buddha, and We
Laura S.
Foreword by Sylvia Boorstein

"A heartfelt and moving description of one person's spiritual journey through the mutually supportive practices of the 12-step program and the teachings of the Buddha."—Arinna Weisman, coauthor, *The Beginner's Guide to Insight Meditation*

Let Go
A Buddhist Guide to Breaking Free of Habits
Martine Batchelor

"A marvelous work: warm, wise, personal, original and eminently practical."—Mark Epstein, MD, author of *Going to Pieces without Falling Apart*

Minding What Matters
Psychotherapy and the Buddha Within
Robert Langan
Foreword by Robert Coles

"This jewel of a book marks the emergence of an important new voice in the field. Langan writes with the wisdom of someone steeped in the practice of both Buddhism and psychoanalysis and the sensibility of a poet."—Jeremy D. Safran, editor of *Psychoanalysis and Buddhism: An Unfolding Dialogue*

How to Be Sick
A Buddhist-Inspired Guide for the Chronically Ill and Their Caregivers
Toni Bernhard
Foreword by Sylvia Boorstein

"Full of hopefulness and promise . . . this book is a perfect blend of inspiration and encouragement. Toni's engaging teaching style shares traditional Buddhist wisdom in a format that is accessible to all readers."—*Huffington Post*